HORIZONS

HORIZONS

Paul H. Dunn

Bookcraft
Salt Lake City, Utah

Library of Congress Catalog Card Number: 81-65718
ISBN 0-88494-424-7

First Printing, 1981

Lithographed in the United States of America
PUBLISHERS PRESS
Salt Lake City, Utah

Acknowledgments

Eternal principles properly applied always help us achieve new horizons. The chapters in this volume contain many truths that when properly applied bring new insight and joy.

As in any publication I am indebted to many. First to my able secretary, Sharene M. Hansen, who in her usual, capable manner typed the manuscript. To Maurine Ward and Sue Kesler for their wonderful ability of expression.

Finally to my wife, Jeanne, for her devoted support and encouragement, and to my daughters, Janet, Marsha, Kellie and their families for constant encouragement.

—PAUL H. DUNN

Contents

Perspective

Part 1

Facades

Did you ever build a sand castle or a house of match sticks? You can spend hours designing, building, adding; but you *know* what the end will be — that house or castle *has* to fall: it can't last.

Remember the time and effort you invested in learning to shoot marbles or play jacks? What a struggle it was to acquire those skills! What practice it took to refine and perfect them! And what do you do with them now? What return do you have on that investment? That time and effort are gone, irretrievably spent on useless skills — a pile of match sticks, a puddle of sand.

I'm not trying to imply that playing the games of childhood means wasting your youth. But I do want you to think about a game we sometimes play as adults which absorbs our time and attention and — in the long run — brings us nothing. That game is building a facade — an act to convince the world that we are better than we really are.

You know what a facade is: it's a false front. All the frontier towns of the nineteenth century had them, and today all the Hollywood sets representing those towns have them again. Imagine the main street of Dodge City or Carson City as you see it on TV: a three-story hotel here, a big old saloon there, the bank across the street, the dry-goods store on the corner — all of them substantial enough buildings to do business in and to support the two or three outlaws who may be hiding on the roof until the shoot-out. It's a real town, right? Wrong! All you have to do is step through the door of one of those buildings and find yourself nowhere to realize that the whole "town" is nothing. It's made up of single-wall store fronts and what *you* imagine to be behind them. Disappointing, isn't it, to find out it's really all facade?

Many of us try to make Hollywood sets of our lives. These are the people who go beyond the natural desire to present their best to the world around them; they create images that are something else, something *besides* the passably humble truth about themselves. And the really sad part about it is this: too often they put so much effort into perfecting that image, that facade, that they neglect their real selves. They build false fronts and have no time or energy left to build real people or real relationships. Once you see through the facade, it's just like Hollywood — disappointing, *nothing.*

You've seen such people. There's the couple with two sets of manners — one for the public and another for at home. Any time they have an audience they are gracious and charming, warm to one another, wise and patient with their children. But once they are alone, the kind words and the pretty gestures disappear, and it's apparent that the relationship is as empty as the spot behind the door to the dry-goods store on that Hollywood set.

Then there's the one who must convince everybody that he's smarter and more knowledgeable on any subject than anyone else. Always talking, always trying to impress, this fellow robs himself of a chance to *become* as well-informed as he wants to appear by refusing to be taught, refusing to listen.

But such a facade can be detected, and once your act is discovered it usually works against you rather than for you. I know an executive who is always on guard for the looks-smarter-than-he-is fellow we've been talking about. This man will never hire a young person who does not have the courage to say "I don't know," because, as he says, a person has to admit that he does not know something before he can find it out. With this man, at least, saving face might mean losing a job.

In almost every case, a facade will ultimately break down. Sooner or later somebody sees through it and feels let down, cheated of what he thought was really there. Could you look someone in the eye knowing he knew you had tried to trick him with an act? It is much easier to get along on what is genuinely *you* than to be exposed as a fraud.

And even if you could fool the people around you indefinitely, you cannot fool yourself and you cannot fool your Lord; he knows you, inside and out. Do you know what he said about facades? Listen to this powerful language; try to see the pictures he paints: "Woe unto you, scribes and Pharisees, hypocrites! for ye make clean the outside of the cup and of the platter, but within they are full of extortion and excess.

"Woe unto you, . . . for ye are like unto whited sepulchres, which indeed appear beautiful outward, but are within full of dead men's bones, and of all uncleanness.

"Even so ye outwardly appear righteous unto men, but within ye are full of hypocrisy and iniquity." (Matthew 23:25, 27-28.)

What you really are, deep down inside, eventually will show itself. And that's okay. You may not be perfect, but you are a child of God; and if you have the courage to be simply yourself, your genuine good qualities will shine through.

There was once a fifteen-year-old girl who worked for a milliner in London. Hers was not a glamorous job, and she went about it humbly and did her best. One day she was sent to deliver a hat to a fine house in Belgrave Square. The butler let her in and left her waiting in the hallway. After a few minutes the lady of the house appeared and, looking startled, said: "I beg your pardon. I'd no idea there was company; I was told there was a delivery here."

"I'm Edith, ma'am, from the milliner's."

"How extraordinary!" came the reply, "who'd have thought they'd send a lady?"

"Oh, I'm not a lady, ma'am," said Edith.

The woman smiled at Edith as she accepted the hat and said: "Not a lady? Well, we know better than that."

Edith made no pretense to be anything but what she was — the milliner's girl. But her true character had shone through somehow, and the woman in Belgrave Square recognized the qualities that helped that fifteen-year-old girl become Dame Edith Evans.

We cannot deny the potential greatness that is in us, but we can lose it if we cover it, with our faults, behind a giant facade. Nor can we correct our faults or learn from them or improve and grow away from them if we try to ignore them. Christ's advice to the Pharisees is valid for us: ". . . cleanse first that which is within the cup and platter, that the outside of them may be clean also." (Matthew 23:26.)

A facade isn't worth the time and effort it takes to build and maintain. Turn your efforts from your image to your essence, make the real you shine as brightly as you'd like the ideal you to shine. You can do it if you admit where you really are and start there.

If the Price Is Right

Psychologists say that people who are seeking success typically choose TV talk shows to watch; they like to identify with the celebrities interviewed on such programs. The celebrities have "made it big," and the success-seeker listens for some clue to help him realize his own dreams. Wouldn't it be grand if we could count on that to work? Imagine tuning in the television to find the secret key to the fulfillment of your wildest hopes.

None of us believes it is quite that simple, but most of us get a little discouraged when we find out how really difficult it is to attain great success. We *want* some shortcut, some clue to link us with our dreams. We know we could be stars or make millions if we just got the right break to start us out.

Children's literature repeats an important truth about winning life's big prizes. Remember the prince in *Sleeping Beauty*? He knew that the very fairest maiden who had ever lived lay sleeping in the castle tower. She was his if he could just reach her, but between them and all around the castle grew a hedge of cruel thorns. To reach the princess, he had to hack his way through the hedge; and with each stroke of his sword the thorns grew thicker and more threatening. Many men had tried to reach the beauty sleeping in the castle, but all had despaired and given up trying to defeat those thorns. In a similar manner Jack, of beanstalk fame, finds a tremendous treasure in the sky sufficient to save and support his starving mother. But the treasure is not his for the taking; it is guarded by a vicious giant whose intent is to make a meal of Jack. To have the treasure, Jack must somehow overcome the giant.

So it is in life: the big prizes are guarded by the fiercest giants. We all want lovely homes, fine families, material wealth, success and recognition in our jobs; but it is only those who are willing to take on and overcome the tremendous challenges which precede such prizes that are destined to win them. We have to pledge our hearts to the battle. We must be willing to get our hands dirty and our faces sweaty with the work. If we expect to have the big prizes, we face and fight the fierce giants. The mild and moderate giants, the tough but not overwhelming thorn hedges, guard only the so-so prizes in life.

And because the challenges are truly taxing, the world is full of would-be's. You know them: the would-be author whose novel is still in his head; the would-be doctor who just couldn't make himself study hard enough in high school and college and so didn't make it to medical school; the would-be millionaire who simply could not make himself save every month when he first started out; the would-be athlete who found training too restrictive; the would-be pianist whose practice time got shorter and shorter.

I know a little girl who started taking violin lessons. The day she got her violin she was so excited she showed it to everybody in the neighborhood. No one could doubt her enthusiasm. Each day she practiced; and when her little friends called to ask her to come and play outside, she would agree to go only after she had finished that hour of practice. Her parents were delighted and began to dream of her first concert tour in a few years.

But then this little girl began to complain that the tender tips of her fingers hurt when she tried to hold down the strings. And of course it was true—those tight strings did cut into her little finger tips, and it was painful. The accomplished violinist has toughened up his fingers and the strings don't bother him any more, but our beginner had such sore hands that before long she gave up the violin.

Any of us can find good reasons to give up on any venture, because any great dream in its unfolding demands intense labor and sacrifice. Those thorny hedges and awful giants between us and our goals are real and frightening and painful. No wonder we get discouraged. But we cannot have the treasures of success unless we surmount those barriers. That is a law of life that never changes.

You have heard the expression "sour grapes." Do you know that it comes from one of Aesop's fables? It is the story of a fox who crept into a vineyard where the sun-ripened grapes hung thick and sweet and luscious from the vines. He longed for a taste, but the trellises held the grapes high above the ground. The fox jumped as high as he could; he backed away and ran and jumped again, stretching and snapping at the grapes. But he could not reach them. When he was tired and hot and discouraged he turned away and, instead of acknowledging his own failure, he muttered: "I never wanted those old grapes anyway. They're probably sour and may have worms as well."

Does the fox fool you with his words? Does he fool himself? Deep inside we know it's a weak excuse that he offers, but many of us do the same thing: we quit and pretend that the fault is in the prize and not in our ability to gain it.

This is no solution at all, because life's big prizes *are* beautiful and good and worthy of our greatest efforts. Of all the prizes offered to us, there is none more dear than eternal life with the Lord. It is the biggest and best prize; it requires the biggest sacrifice and the best efforts of our lives. We are foolish if we think it can be had for anything less than our supreme effort, our ultimate sacrifice, our greatest will.

"If thou wilt be perfect," said Jesus to the rich young man, "go and sell that thou hast, and give to the poor, and thou shalt have treasure in heaven: and come and follow me." (Matthew 19:21.) To gain eternal life with our Father in Heaven means we must be willing, if called upon, to sacrifice all things for his cause. We must be willing to sacrifice even our dearest weaknesses, those sins we are loath to part with.

To obtain the level of righteousness necessary to enter the kingdom of God demands the greatest effort we ever give to anything. How could it be any less? It is the best treasure of all, and it is guarded by the fierce giants of our own weaknesses — giants that must be met with courage and patience and an unbending drive to succeed. It is not a goal for the fainthearted, but it is one we all desire. May each of us have the courage to give his heart to pursuing it.

Up a Tree

At one time or another we have all been asked: "What would you do if Christ were to return today? What if he came to your door —would you be ashamed to invite him into your home?" We have thought about the question, perhaps, and then tossed it aside as irrelevant at the moment. But I'd like to suggest that this is *not* a "what if" proposition. For those of us who profess to be Christians this is a very real circumstance: Christ is currently asking to be admitted to our homes and included in our lives. The important question is how we respond to him.

Do you panic when the phone rings and a long-lost friend says he's just arrived in town and will be at your door in twenty minutes? An unexpected arrival is likely to throw any of us into a frenzy of tidying up and quick preparation. Even anticipated guests usually mean a last-minute rush to be sure everything is ready. If we know the Lord is eagerly waiting to be invited into our lives, why then don't we hurry to make room? Why are we not prepared? Why do we hesitate to hustle things into shape for him?

The story is told of a time when Daniel Webster found himself the unexpected guest of a rather unconcerned host —one who was perhaps not unlike many of us in his lack of enthusiastic welcome. It seems that Webster had spent his day hunting, and his quest had taken him a considerable distance from the inn where he'd been staying. As dusk deepened, it became pretty apparent that he could not make it back that night, so he began to look for a place to stay until morning. He trudged through the woods until —quite a while after dark —he came upon a farmhouse. Webster pounded on the door until an upstairs window was raised. The sleepy-eyed farmer thrust his head out of the window and called, "What do you want?"

"I want to stay the night here," replied Webster.

"Fine," said the farmer, "stay there." Slam went the window.

One of my favorite stories in the Bible is about a rather different host. When Jesus on his way to Jerusalem passed through Jericho, a large crowd gathered and pressed about him. Zacchaeus, who was chief among the publicans and therefore very rich, also wanted to see Jesus. But because he was a short man he could not see past the crowd, so he ran ahead and climbed up a sycamore tree to get a better view. Imagine a tax collector, neither liked nor trusted by the people, forgetting his dignity and bounding up a tree like an enthusiastic boy.

When Jesus came by, says the scripture, he looked up and saw Zacchaeus and said, "Zacchaeus, make haste, and come down; for to day I must abide at thy house." (Luke 19:5.) Now, that pretty well put Zacchaeus on the spot; but, as we shall see, he came through like a champ because he was ready: he believed Jesus would come, and he was seeking Jesus even as he came.

Suppose the Lord beckoned you from your tree to share your home with him. Would you be caught short as the short Zacchaeus was not? Could you include Jesus in your family routine, in your entertainment, in your reading, in your conversation? Wouldn't you like a little lead time to prime your kids and practice holding your temper and dust behind the bookcase? Of course you would. And here's the irony: if you call yourself a Christian, you profess to beckon the Lord at all times, not to hold him back until you are ready for him. I can't believe that any of us would really slam the window down and say, "Give me a while to think about it," if we knew the Lord was standing at our doors. So if we're not seriously making ready for him, perhaps we simply don't believe he wants to come into our hearts.

There are lots of things we don't *really* believe: our behavior gives us away no matter what we say. For example, nobody believes a restaurant is really interested in his comments and suggestions. Nobody believes the suggestion box at work really acts as a communication link between management and labor. Nobody believes you when you say you were just about to write a letter or your car had a flat tire or you watch only educational television. Nobody believes a contractor's first estimate, nobody believes there's really a gas shortage, nobody believes the sign on the door that says *pull*. At least, nobody *acts* as if he believed these things.

And, unfortunately, very few act as if they believe Christ were standing ready at the door — ready to ease pain and give comfort and make all things clear. If we truly believed it, we'd be ready, we'd be out seeking Christ, we'd be at the city gates staked out in a tree to be sure we couldn't miss him. Such a man was Zacchaeus, who came down as the Lord asked him to do and "received him joyfully."

Now, when the people saw whom Jesus had chosen to stay with, they murmured because Zacchaeus was a sinner. But Zacchaeus put his belief into action right away: "Behold, Lord, the half of my goods I give to the poor; and if I have taken any thing from any man by false accusation, I restore him fourfold." And Jesus immediately rewarded him, saying, "This day is salvation come to this house." (Luke 19:8-9.)

Isn't that great? Zacchaeus not only believed Jesus was there, he also went out to meet him, and he repented. He allowed the Savior's influence to change his life.

When we, like Zacchaeus, seek Christ's influence, when we invite him into our lives, we place ourselves in a position to receive all the good gifts he offers us. Let us not slam the window shut; let us not doubt that he stands ready to bless us. Let us instead welcome him, going forth to let him into our lives and accepting his invitation: "Come unto me, all ye that labour and are heavy laden, and I will give you rest." (Matthew 11:28.)

The Crowd Pleasers

Everybody loves to be loved, to feel the approval and support of other people. A baby thrives on his family's cheers for his first steps, a child struggles for acceptance among his playmates, a student takes satisfaction in a good grade, an athlete strives for acceptance on a team, a business person works toward a raise or promotion, a parent hopes for the word of thanks that means his love and concern are returned by his children. All of these are examples of people needing the pat on the back that says: "I approve of you. You belong." Every one of us needs such reassurance: it is our reward and our encouragement to go on; it serves us just as applause serves a performer.

It is good for us to give and to receive support from one another in this manner. But, as with all positive forces, this can work to our detriment if it is misdirected. As we try to be crowd pleasers, we can easily put our values in the hands of the crowd and thereby lose control of them. Suppose, for example, that the athlete striving for a place on a team finds himself among fellows who break training to go partying. His personal values may dictate that he obey the training rules; but if he does that, will the guys on the team ever really accept him? He can't please the crowd *and* himself. To solve this dilemma, one value or the other will have to go.

You've seen this kind of peer pressure a hundred times. You've known people who cheated just a little on income tax or who took a drink, laughed at a dirty joke, or made a cutting remark because everybody seemed to be doing it. Alone, a person may have no difficulty defining and following his own values; but it is something quite different to be the single small voice in the crowd to say: "This is not right. This is not the way I want to behave." Nevertheless, there is no excuse for *your* compromising *your* values for *any* crowd.

The topic of peer pressure always reminds me of Peter, Christ's disciple. If ever there was a loyal and trusting follower, it was Peter. At one point in his ministry Christ asked his disciples what men thought of him, whom they thought he was. And his disciples answered that some thought he was John the Baptist and some thought he was Elias or another of the prophets. Then, in earnest because it was important to him that at least his own disciples recognize him, Jesus asked, "But whom say ye that I am?" And of all of them, it was Peter who spoke: "Thou art the Christ, the Son of the living God." (Matthew 16:15.)

Later, when Jesus walked on the water of Galilee, it was Peter who trusted enough to step out on the waves toward him while the others watched from the ship. Peter had courage and faith; there is no question about it.

And yet when Jesus was taken and persecuted the night before the crucifixion, Peter followed at a safe distance and stayed outside the high priest's palace. We can only speculate as to whether Peter could hear the commotion as Jesus was questioned and accused, slapped and spit upon, mocked and ridiculed. But we do know that, as Peter sat there, a young woman said to him, "Thou also wast with Jesus of Galilee." And Peter denied it, loudly enough for all to hear, just as Jesus had told him he would do before morning. Peter got up then and walked out onto the porch, where another woman saw him and told the crowd there that he had been with Jesus. This time Peter denied it with an oath and said, "I do not know the man." Finally the group approached Peter, saying they knew from his speech that he was one of Jesus' followers; and Peter cursed and swore and said, "I know not the man." (See Matthew 26:58-75.)

Even faithful Peter gave in to the pressure of the crowd. And in spite of the many times he had stood firm and spoken up loyally for the Lord, he was bitterly regretful of that one slip. Matthew eloquently records that after the third denial "immediately the cock crew. And Peter remembered the word of Jesus, which said unto him, Before the cock crow, thou shalt deny me thrice. And he went out, and wept bitterly." (Matthew 26:74-75.)

Had Peter been true to himself and his Lord, had he stood up for what he knew was right, could any crowd have caused him as much pain as his own heart now caused him?

Peter was a great and good disciple, and much was expected of him. I myself saw crowd pressure dash the hopes of another man of whom much was expected.

It was on a college campus. This young man had been a dedicated and serious Christian, but he had set his activities in his church aside as he became more involved in school and in his fraternity. Still, his reputation included his Christian ideals.

During initiation this fellow's fraternity, like the others, subjected their pledges to some hazing—a series of small tortures, tasks and pranks which the pledges must go through in order to become active members. All fraternities and sororities do it; everybody gets involved; and so did this particular young man.

He was one of seven boys who surrounded a young initiate and demanded that he swallow a piece of liver with a string attached to it. What a joke it was to yank that piece of string and bring the liver back up to be swallowed again! Did that brother who had professed Christianity have second thoughts about participating in this scene? If he did, he failed to voice them; and his silence cost him dearly. The pledge choked on the liver and died in the midst of the party.

Besides their personal grief, the seven fraternity brothers had to bear trials in the civil courts and at their school. At the tribunal held on campus each of them was interrogated and forced to repeat every detail of the incident for a jury of his peers. The college court suspended six of the boys for a year; but the seventh, the Christian, was expelled from the school forever.

I was present that day, and I couldn't resist questioning those in charge about the apparent inequity of the verdict. They agreed that all seven were equally guilty; but, they said, the religious boy went against his deepest convictions to join in the stunt. "He is no leader," said the school administration. "We have no room for anyone who can so quickly and easily compromise his own conscience." So much for following the crowd.

You know what you believe in, and your friends and family and neighbors and fellow workers know it too. Your own self-respect and clear conscience cannot be brought back as easily as you may trade them away by not being true to what you believe is right. Speak your convictions. Deny not Jesus Christ because you are timid. Dare to stand alone if necessary, knowing you will not have to stand ashamed before the Lord and those who know what you profess. The Lord loves those who are willing to join the fray and to stand up for themselves and for him.

May each of us have the courage to raise his voice for the right, especially when it may be one lonely voice.

Perspective

There is a story about two ancient Greek sculptors who competed for the honor of having their work displayed in the public square. Each was skilled, and each wanted his statue in the place of honor. The first was meticulous, smoothing and polishing the stone until each feature was distinct. His work looked so nearly like a real human face that even those who examined it most closely declared they thought it might speak. The second sculptor appeared to have given up in the face of so formidable a competitor. His statue was crude, the lines jagged and unrefined, the stone rough. It was hard to discern in it a human figure at all. So the first man's statue was placed in the square where all could see it.

But, high on its pedestal, it was too far away for the people to appreciate its detail. Indeed, it was so blurred by the distance that it could not be seen clearly from any angle. At last they removed it and put in its place the second artist's work — the one that was so crude. Viewed from a distance, this piece took on such vitality and life that it was considered a creation of great beauty, and its creator was praised as a man of genius and clever imagination.

Sometimes it is not easy to see truth, in art or in life, and especially about our own decisions in life. We're just too close to our own concerns to see them properly. Much as we want to believe ourselves to be wise and farsighted, most of us base our responses to life on the pressures of the moment — on the immediate crisis rather than the long-range issue.

How many men and women all but forsake their spouses and families for achievement in their careers? How many moms and dads are so meticulous about the house, the car, and the yard that they forget to notice the children who live there? How many students let their social activities become more important than their education? And how many times have *you* given in to a moment's emotion and let loose with an angry speech that moments later you can tell has caused some serious hurt?

It happens again and again with all of us. We live in the here and now, and each moment crackles with its own urgent demands. Too often our responses to those demands are hasty — we go for the laugh or we snap back to provide relief of our anger or entertainment for our friends or diversion from the underlying problem. Unfortunately, it is *after* we respond that we think through the implications — and then it's too late.

Now, the Lord tells us that "truth is knowledge of things as they are, and as they were, and as they are to come." (D&C 93:24.) Life has meaning and consistency that extends far beyond the present. The Lord also makes a distinction between "things temporal" and "things spiritual." The word *temporal* implies the limitations of time — "things temporal" have the rather disconcerting property of being here today and gone tomorrow. And that's okay, as long as we remember that these things *are* fleeting and as long as we treat them accordingly, investing in them no more time or effort or love than they merit. Pouring your soul or the precious hours of your life into achieving temporal goals is like blowing your whole paycheck on cotton candy: it may taste good for an instant, but once the moment's pleasure is past there's nothing more — nothing at all to swallow.

Think of the very early Christians who faced the jaws of the hungry lions in the Roman coliseums. It must have been difficult for them to stand by their beliefs with such a horrible death as the consequence. Think how much easier life was for the Roman nobles who basked in the glory of their power as they ordered such slaughters and watched them for casual amusement. Of course, from our perspective in time we can see that the Roman Empire eventually fell, and its leaders — however great or small — met their own ends, taking with them only the rewards of their way of life. They trusted the moment, while the Christians they tortured put their confidence in principles and truths that no death or passage of time could alter. Neither the Roman nor the Christian had the advantage of our perspective on his place in history, but — in faith — one of them chose to base his choices on an eternal rather than a finite time-table.

Ultimately, eternity is the timetable for all men. And it is with *this* perspective that we must make our life choices. Which clock — the temporal or the eternal — do you measure your life by? I don't mean just on Sundays or in other quiet moments when you catch your breath and contemplate; any of us can do well under those circumstances — just as anybody can reflect on the grandeur of all creation when he gazes at the Grand Canyon. I am asking how you measure and choose when you are caught in a traffic jam or when you have the opportunity to hurt someone who opposes you. What then? Do you consider the eternal implications of your actions and words, or do you focus on whatever you want to accomplish right at the moment? You know, a temporal success can be an eternal disaster.

You trade success now for long-range failure if you are working on a lower principle when a higher one lies before you. You trade success for failure any time your work does not build your character and challenge you to seek loftier goals. When your purpose in working is limited to the acquiring of financial wealth and physical comfort, your success at work is buying you failure to realize your potential as a human being. When your career success costs you your good health, when it requires that you crush the next fellow's dream or cloud his hope, when it draws you away from your family, when it focuses your attention away from your friends and toward money and possessions, then that success is really a failure.

Most important, whether you are a lawyer or a merchant, a laborer or a teacher, any time your role in your work overshadows your nature, your spontaneous self, then that successful role is making a failure of the whole person. Success now can be the first step toward a failure farther reaching and much more significant than you can possibly imagine; because from where you stand at any given moment in your life, your perspective is limited. Like the Greek citizens who couldn't adequately judge the statues, you might easily choose a course of action which honestly appears wholesome and productive to you now but which, viewed from a greater distance and with greater wisdom, actually shows itself sinister.

How can you surmount this difficulty? How can you hope to see with greater scope than is available to you? How can you resist the daily temporal pressures of life? Primarily by understanding their temporal nature. One man says that whenever he is tempted to place greater importance on an immediate concern than on an eternal one, all he does is envision white rats running through a maze, learning how to win that immediate reward by practicing its pursuit. Laboratory rats are easily conditioned by various stimuli to behave in a certain manner. Even single cell amoebas respond to touch. With those pictures in mind, can't we choose to *act* rather than *be acted upon* by circumstance?

It is time each of us gave up chasing his daily routine long enough to get his bearings and figure out what direction to follow. If we do not choose a course from the vantage point of an eternal point of view, we can be certain of arriving eventually in some dead-end street bewildered as to how we got there. Of course, the answer to that question will be that for a long, long time we were following a course which could lead us nowhere else.

May we cultivate eternal perspective; may we have the wisdom to see the implications beyond this immediate decision, distinguishing between temporal and eternal success; may we have the courage always to stand up for what we know.

All by Myself

Once there was a man who stepped too near a cliff and fell off. You can imagine the fast and mighty praying he did as he hurtled toward the ground. "Please, God," he cried, "save me! Get me out of this, and I promise I'll do whatever you say for the rest of my life." Suddenly he jerked to a stop — mid-air — and looked around to see his shirt tail caught on a branch protruding from the canyon wall. "Whew!" he sighed. "Never mind the prayer, Lord — I've got it under control."

Ever notice yourself acting like that? Most of us do — we pray earnestly for success at work or harmony at home or safety in travel, and when things work out for us we pat ourselves on the back: "Boy, I really worked for this," or "It's a good thing I've developed such good judgment."

In the midst of inflation, many of us are turning to do-it-yourself projects to save money. We grow some of our own food, we learn to repair the car ourselves, we paint, we bottle fruit, we bake bread, we do our own plumbing. All of these are commendable efforts — we should be as self-sufficient as we can be. But we can't be totally independent — life is not a do-it-yourself, easy-to-assemble, satisfaction-guaranteed project in a kit. Life is too complicated an endeavor for anyone to handle alone.

Remember how you smile at the child who declares, "I can tie my shoes all by myself," and proceeds to make a mess of the shoe-laces for fifteen minutes? Or the one who insists, "Me do it," at meals and manages to spoon food all over everything in the room? A child doesn't fool you with these assertions, but his pride in accomplishing such chaos *does* amuse you—unless you're the one who has to clean up. Why do we smile? Because the innocent attitude that he can handle it is obviously unfounded and serves only to point out his childish fantasies.

What's the difference in maturity between the child who insists on doing it himself and the adult who similarly will not accept help? Oh, yes, there are many of us—we're afraid to admit to a vulnerability, a lack of control over the situation. Sometimes we're ashamed to ask for help, believing that it will label us forever as weak. But the simple fact is that every one of us needs the others at some time for something. None of us is totally self-reliant—nor should we try to be.

Think for a moment of the variety of goods and services we take for granted that someone will provide for us. Could you supply yourself with gasoline for your car? How long could you do without electricity? What if nobody filled up the chuckholes in the streets or picked up your garbage or brought your mail? Suppose you were suddenly cast back in time a few hundred years—do you have the knowledge and skill to build an engine, make an aspirin, organize a government? Every day we rely on other people, whether living today or already gone, to provide for us in these ways. We accept these kinds of dependence quite casually because they are so very common, and so we often forget how very important the needs they represent are.

Similarly, we too often forget how desperately we need the Lord. He is quite literally the source of energy that allows us life on this planet. Because we take for granted the fact that we exist and function here, we fail to acknowledge the great gift we have in daily sustenance. As King Benjamin so powerfully stated to his people: "I say unto you that if ye should serve him who has created you from the beginning, and is preserving you from day to day, by lending you breath, that ye may live and move and do according to your own will, and even supporting you from one moment to another—I say, if ye should serve him with all your whole souls yet ye would be unprofitable servants." (Mosiah 2:21.)

Do we feel supported minute to minute by the Lord? Something headstrong and proud within tempts us to say no to this idea. Even though we may accept and gratefully acknowledge his help in times of crisis, we resist the notion that we need him just to survive, just to maintain our status as living creatures. Nevertheless it is true, and we must learn to receive humbly and with thanksgiving that which we so arrogantly assume is ours anyway. Certainly it is important for us to give — to one another and to the Lord — our services, our time, our material wealth, our love. But we must not fail to learn also to receive graciously and to recognize our gifts as what they are.

If you doubt this, I invite you to look at the life of Jesus Christ as an example. Surely he gave — his offerings range from the simplest word of praise to the greatest, most incomprehensible sacrifice in the history of mankind. But his is also a story of accepting, of receiving, of relying on others. He alone of all those who have lived on earth could have chosen to live without the administrations of the people around him, but instead he depended on them — a choice which must be viewed as significant.

Jesus Christ's mortal life began as a helpless infant, entirely dependent upon the care of his mother for shelter, food, warmth, and instruction. He went to John the Baptist to receive the ordinance of baptism, insisting against John's protests that he had need of this administration. The Savior, who fed the multitude with a few fish and loaves, relied on others for his own sustenance — he always slept, ate, and resided as a guest in the homes of his followers. Finally, his burial place on the earth he had created was a few square feet in a borrowed tomb. In life and in death Christ gratefully accepted the aid and comfort and graciousness of his friends.

To emphasize the importance of allowing those we love to provide for us, Christ taught this principle by example at the Last Supper. As he bathed the feet of his disciples, he demonstrated his love for them and showed them that, in order for them to understand his love, they must accept this service. When Peter shrank back, declaring, "Thou shalt never wash my feet," Jesus replied, "If I wash thee not, thou hast no part with me." (John 13:8.)

Let us learn to accept the gifts others would render us. Not one of us could survive very well without the others, not one could survive at all without the Lord. Let us then admit our interdependence and rejoice, giving thanks, in the aid and support we daily give and receive. We need one another; let us acknowledge it gratefully.

Lenet Hadley Read suggested in an *Ensign* article that receiving righteously helps us develop loving relationships. She wrote: "It is not enough simply to receive.

"We can receive with greed, thinking only of the gift.

"We can receive with insensitivity, not realizing the cost or sacrifice the gift has caused the giver.

"We can resist humility and love and receive with feelings of disdain for the one who gives.

"We can receive with indifference, as if the ministering is our 'due.' . . .

"Obviously such attitudes are not righteous. Perhaps such attitudes are what have given receiving a bad name.

"The challenge is to receive with humility, with sincere appreciation for the *sacrifice* behind the gift, with common respect for oneself and the giver, and, above all, with the firm knowledge that every gift ultimately comes from the Creator of all things." ("The Other Half of Giving," March 1975, p. 62.)

Every person contributes to your life and to mine, and the Lord who gave us life sustains us in it. Remember Paul's counsel: "And the eye cannot say unto the hand, I have no need of thee: nor again the head to the feet, I have no need of you." (1 Corinthians 12:21.) Let us then accept one another's offerings as graciously as they are presented, and do so giving thanks.

Distractions

How long has it been since you held a newborn baby? Remember how soft that wrinkly pink skin is? Did you notice how that tiny person stared so hard at something just beyond your shoulder? A baby is a miracle all right—a small parcel of humanity who quietly but certainly takes over the house and changes your world. Yesterday you didn't know him; today you defer to him, changing your schedule and seeing that he has the softest bed and is the first one fed. You are fascinated with his miniature hands and feet, his delicate eyelashes, his small but perfect ears. And you sense that he holds some tremendous secret in his little head; you want to hold him close and say: "Where did you come from, little one? Tell me what you know." But when you do, your only answer is an untranslatable cry or an inscrutable smile. You are left to your own devices to find out the babe's secret.

The scriptures, of course, tell us where we all come from. There we learn that before our mortal birth we lived in the very presence of our Heavenly Father. The great poet Wordsworth also caught the truth of our eternal history in this beautiful imagery:

> Our birth is but a sleep and a forgetting:
> The Soul that rises with us, our life's Star,
> Hath had elsewhere its setting,
> And cometh from afar:
> Not in entire forgetfulness,
> And not in utter nakedness,

> But trailing clouds of glory do we come
> From God, who is our home.
> ("Ode: Intimations of Immortality from
> Recollections of Early Childhood.")

The scriptures go beyond this to explain that some among us were great and intelligent, others had special gifts or talents, but all of us wanted to achieve the same goal—to become more like our Father in Heaven. So he called us together in a great council, and there we learned that each of us would have a chance to come to earth and gain a body. Oh, we wouldn't be gone long—earth life is just a blink in the eternal scheme of things. But the catch was that for as long as we were on earth we would have no memory of where we'd been. Mortality was to be an opportunity for us to prove ourselves; and if we could remember all about our premortal existence, mortality wouldn't be a valid test at all.

We were all so excited about this chance to progress that, the Bible says, "the morning stars sang together, and all the sons of God shouted for joy." (Job 38:7.) From the security of our heavenly home and with eternal rather than temporal perspective, we must have thought that mortality wouldn't be all that hard. Maybe we just didn't realize how thoroughly, how utterly, we'd forget where we came from. Perhaps we couldn't imagine how long that earth-blink would *seem*. We came hopefully and enthusiastically. Can't you just hear yourself saying confidently, "Watch me go!"

So now here we are on earth without that memory and perspective, suspecting that the very young know more than they can tell. By the time a child can speak, any glimpse that might have lingered is long gone; and for most of us the idea of our heritage is intriguing but not always real. All those spiritual strivings, all that knowledge and understanding of our eternal purpose are obscured by distractions. You know what I mean—the immediate press of living, the real and important matters of rest and nourishment and work and relationships, take our attention away from contemplation of the eternities. Who has the time or the mental space to meditate without interruption from external or internal voices?

You want to pray to the Lord; in fact, you kneel down with that intention — to pray with such intensity and feeling that all the fog between you is blown away, to pour out your very soul, and, in the quiet that creates, hear his response. But then something comes up. Something small, usually; but something you can't ignore: the phone rings, your children need you, exhaustion clouds your mind, you think suddenly of a way to solve a problem, you remember that you owe a friend a letter. Just like that, your deeper yearnings get swallowed up in ordinary demands.

Or you feel the need to be in touch somehow with yourself, to listen to the quiet messages from your own soul — the kind that come with such clarity and force that you know you didn't make them up. But there is such a lot of noise in the world that you can't hear them. The rhythm of traffic or typewriters or even other people's conversation distracts your thinking, or the sounds of your own ideas or needs or fears thunder through your head — and you just can't cut through it all to hear that inner voice.

Ultimately, we all become a little like the people who work in the constant roar of the factories. The din there becomes so much a part of their lives that they cease to notice it. In some cases factories have issued ear plugs or ear muffs to keep working conditions up to environmental standards, but the workers don't wear them — they are more trouble than the noise they would cut out, and they are harder to ignore. But studies show that after years of working in the jangle of machinery, many people's hearing ability is permanently impaired. For most of them it comes on so gradually that they don't realize their hearing is diminished any more than they notice all the accustomed sounds of the factory. They can be missing all the music of the world around them and never even be aware of it.

We, too, can become so used to the noise and distractions of mortality that we cease to hear those vitally important eternal whisperings. And the longer we go between tuning in to them, the greater the chances are that our ability to do so will falter. When was the last time you really focused in on that fleeting something at the outskirts of memory that reminds you that you were meant for more than earth can ever provide you? It is the ordinariness of life that blunts our best hopes.

In C. S. Lewis's brilliant book *The Screwtape Letters* there is a clear illustration of this. The premise of the book is that an apprentice tempter and his experienced mentor are exchanging letters on the subject of perfecting methods for leading their human "patients" carefully down to hell. The older devil at one point tells of a man he'd been working on for twenty years. The man liked to go to the library to read; and one day as he was reading, one of those eternal glimmers started leading his thoughts toward some important truths.

As you may imagine, this upset the devil a good deal; after all, twenty years is a long time to work on one project. A clever tempter, he knew there was no point in arguing or trying to inject a counter-thought into his patient's mind. Instead, he whispered that it was lunch time, that such great ideas as this man had stumbled upon could be better understood if he came back to them rested after a meal. As soon as the man started for the library door, the devil knew he had won. On the street people hurried along, the newsboy on the corner shouted the day's headlines, and the traffic roared by. Another whisper and the patient was striding up the block thinking that too much contemplation might not be as good as a dose of real life. The glimmer was gone; the tempter was victorious. All he had needed was some everyday noise.

Every one of us can count on getting a sizeable dose of real life here on earth whether we seek it or not. Daily problems and the demands for food and rest and comfort that our bodies make all draw us away from pursuing our loftiest thoughts. Because that is true—because the answer to that question I asked earlier is "Nobody, nobody has time to meditate"—it is crucial that we *make* time every day for quiet contemplation. We need to get to know ourselves, our God, the nature of our own high origin—and that knowledge doesn't come when we are running at top speed.

Just as a river's white water can tell us something of the ocean it runs toward, so the voices within us can tell us of the greater dimensions of our destinies. But only if we *listen*, only if we make an effort to turn down the noise in our lives and tune in our own souls. We can never hear those voices, never catch those glimmers of eternal life, if we allow ourselves to be carried along with the flood of daily concerns. Heed the counsel of the Lord to David: "Be still, and know that I am God." (Psalm 46:10.) The two go together; you must create the stillness to have the knowledge.

Government by the People

One United States senator formally requested of his constituents their ideas about which federal laws were most useless. Did he get an earful! His office was inundated with mail from his state and many others—this was the chance hundreds had been waiting for to gripe where they just might be heard. Government was described as an "abominable paperwork monster," and many cries were made to return the governing of this nation to its people.

We all like to sound off. But, you know, in the final analysis *we* are the people who determine what government does—by our votes, by our contributions in time and money, by our relative involvement, by how much we ignore, by what we know and do about effecting change. All our complaints eventually must come home to us. What kind of a citizen are you?

For example, consider your involvement in the electoral process. Most of us are guilty of walking into the voting booth poorly prepared, and so we mark at least part of the ballot by guesswork. In fact, in most local elections it is almost predictable that the candidate whose name falls first in the alphabet and is therefore probably listed first on the ballot will be the winner. That's not government by *people*—it's more like government by alphabet soup. And heaven help the Zabriskie who runs for office in that system!

The fact is that being informed well enough to make intelligent choices takes time and study and thought. Most of us are too busy to invest all that in an election, even though we may have plenty of enthusiasm to put into complaining when the people we elected aren't doing what we want them to. Even if we don't vote at all, we influence the kind of representative we get—silence at the polls implies agreement. If you *didn't* vote for the person or policy you disagree with, you have no right to criticize unless you *did* vote against. Always remember that there are people working actively for a way of life you might not want; and unless you oppose them, you may have to abide by their decisions. By the same token, those people and principles you very much favor require your support, not your silence. Indifference can squelch the greatest of ideas and encourage the worst.

Some of us argue that a single vote or voice would make no difference anyway. They say: "I am only one. I have no impact on this society—why should I bother?" But consider these cases. In 1645 one vote gave Oliver Cromwell control of England. In 1776 one vote determined that English, not German, would be the official language of the United States. In 1923 one vote put Hitler in control of the Nazi party. In 1941—just two weeks before Pearl Harbor was bombed—one vote saved selective service. Imagine what it would mean to have been "only one" in any of these situations!

Your voice can make an impact too. In fact, if you'd lived in the old West as a pioneer, you'd hardly have had the option to stay on the fringes of community affairs. In the desert communities where water was as precious as gold dust, people survived only by growing crops dependent entirely on irrigation, bringing water from streams in nearby mountains. The rule was a simple one: If you didn't help build the irrigation system, your family didn't get any of the water it brought. That's what I call motivation—instant community involvement. When schools were built, if you wanted your children to have an education you paid the teacher personally, often in kind. The teacher might receive a chicken, a pound of wheat, anything an anxious parent could find to insure his child's education. Such a system got a parent involved in schools and school policy quicker than any of today's room-mother assignments ever could. After all, he may have placed a chicken (never mind the child) on the line.

So what about today? Where can you and I make a difference in our complex, fast-moving world? The place to begin is where you have the most influence—in your own community, dealing with local problems. Oh, I know it would be much more exciting to confer with the President or to give the United Nations the solution to world hunger. But the reality is that most of us won't have those opportunities; and the world's gravest problems have their counterparts or perhaps even their roots in our own communities where we *do* have a chance to help. Crime, juvenile delinquency, child abuse, unemployment — all are national ills that have their manifestations in your own town, right where you can make a real contribution to the cure. All you need to do is look around you to find a worthy project. Clean up a neighborhood, improve library services, start a campaign to cut pollution. No matter where you live, there is some public problem that needs your attention.

In one small city a group of citizens became concerned about the spread of pornography. More and more of what had been the better theaters in town were showing cheap X-rated movies. Supermarkets and other variety stores frequented by children displayed lewd magazines. It seemed that part of the downtown area was decaying due to the theater clientele. Finally, just a handful of people went to local officials and asked that the laws regarding these establishments be carefully reviewed to see if they met community standards. They presented careful arguments in favor of a city prosecutor who would concentrate on issues of pornography. They talked to managers in the stores they frequented to ask if certain kinds of material they considered offensive couldn't be moved off open display.

The result? The number of theaters in town showing pornographic movies was reduced from six to one. Throughout the area, stores cooperated by moving certain kinds of material off open display. The downtown area became respectable and safe. It was only a handful of people who accomplished these things. But it was a handful of people who cared and who did their homework so they approached their goals rationally and not emotionally. It was a handful of people who were not afraid to get involved.

The responsibility of maintaining our standard of living, of defending our rights, of protecting our precious liberties lies squarely with us. It is a sacred duty. Remember "that governments were instituted of God for the benefit of man; and that he holds men accountable for their acts in relation to them, both in making laws and administering them, for the good and safety of society." (D&C 134:1.)

Whatever your personal political persuasion, whatever your concern, *now* is the time to make your voice heard in the affairs of society. Edmund Burke was correct when he said, "All that is necessary for the triumph of evil is that good men do nothing."

Kindness

Part 2

Courtesy—Never Out of Style

Observers of society say that manners are in a state of transition. Nobody's quite sure what good manners are any more. A hundred years ago, even twenty-five years ago, young boys and girls learned to say "Yes, Ma'am" and "No, Sir." They learned to call all adults "Miss" or "Mrs." or "Mr." But that's not the case any more. Today's kids are likely to answer a question with a drooping, "Yeah," or, "Nope." When they don't like something, many are likely to wrinkle up their noses and say, "It stinks." And in the wake of the women's movement, every gentleman has asked himself the question, "Should I open the door for the lady, or will she think it's insulting"? Most often the answer to that depends entirely on the lady involved.

So what is courtesy these days? Is it simply a lost art, a relic from a history museum? Is it something to be donned like a hat just for special occasions? We've all heard the expression, "Put on your best manners." Does that assume we can put them off just as easily?

Let's look at the evidence. An old man, his arms laden with packages, tried to negotiate his way out through the revolving doors of a large department store. Nothing seemed to work. He and his packages together were too bulky to make it through the door, but he was afraid to leave half of them and make two trips. Suppose the packages were stolen? Who noticed his plight? How many hurrying customers passed him by and shoved their way through the doors without a backward glance? Well over twenty people came scurrying by him and just didn't see.

Here's another package story. One woman saw another woman coming from a parking lot into a building with her arms loaded. The first woman stopped, taking an extra minute of her time to wait and hold the door for the heavily burdened second woman. But the second woman wasn't as gracious. She breezed by without even a "thank you" for the courteous gesture.

I know a woman who was coming from the hospital after having minor surgery. She couldn't afford a taxi and didn't have a car, so what was her choice as a stranger in a new city? She waited on the corner by the hospital for the bus to come. When it came she pulled her suitcase wearily behind her onto the bus. Of course, the bus was full — not a single seat left — and she, just three days from surgery, rode standing all the way home. Nobody offered her a seat. Maybe nobody noticed.

You know, if any of us were to be granted an interview with the Queen of England, we would painstakingly prepare to assure that we said just the right thing, that we did just the right thing. We'd read a book on social protocol, polish up our gracious ways. Why should we behave any differently in the way we treat each other? Do we think less of our friends and families than we do of a total stranger, however royal she may be? Are we too hurried, too self-centered to consider those around us? Do those of us who live in big cities, where we travel through so much of our lives anonymously, just assume we can be rude because we may never meet the stranger again? After all, you'll never see that clerk in the store again or the commuter seated near you on the bus. Why be courteous to the man who calls to remind you your credit card payment has not yet arrived?

Samuel Goldwyn said this: "Never act toward someone as though you were never going to come across him again in life. . . . Never sacrifice what the future may hold for some immediate gain. Be yourself with everyone you meet — but be your best self, for you can be sure that before you have lived out your life you are going to meet again. . . . You always meet people a second time." (*Richard Evans' Quote Book*, Publishers Press, p. 172.)

I believe the test of a truly gracious person is how he treats the person who can do nothing for him, maybe even the person he is likely never to see again.

So, how are you going to learn good manners in a world that sometimes seems too hurried to care? There are many people who will give you advice. Library shelves are stacked with books on etiquette that will spell out precisely how to act in social situations. You can easily look up which fork to use and how to prepare a socially correct wedding. There are even codes of etiquette for the socially correct second wedding.

But real courtesy is something that goes far deeper than knowing the socially correct thing to do. Long after any of us has mastered how to eat fried chicken in public, long after we've learned to write the obligatory thank-you note, we may still have to master real graciousness.

It is graciousness that is at the center of this story of a Wyoming ranch family. Bonnie was only about ten years old when her family moved from Salt Lake City to their new ranch just outside of Afton, but she well understood the transition her city-raised mother underwent with that move. Even for family lunches Bonnie's mom could not forego a clean white table cloth and proper place settings at the table.

In the spring of their first year in Wyoming Bonnie's dad had to hire a local boy to help him with calving and repairing fences. Bonnie, as the oldest child, was a great help with daily chores, but the demands of early spring on the range required at least two men. So Roland, a large, lanky fellow of sixteen, came every morning and every afternoon after school.

One afternoon their work lasted until after sundown, so Bonnie's father invited Roland to stay and have supper with the family. There was nothing extraordinary about the meal — meat loaf and green peas, hot rolls and a salad — but Roland was not accustomed to the finely set table. After he had scrubbed his hands and taken his seat he seemed to Bonnie to be out of place. To be sure, as soon as the blessing was said Roland reached for his fork with the rest of them; but immediately it fell from his awkward hand, clattering against his plate. Bonnie watched, surprised and sorry for Roland as time and again he tried to scoop his peas together but succeeded only in scattering them over the rim of the plate. But she was more surprised to see her father set his own fork aside and pile meat loaf, gravy, and peas onto his knife blade and lift the whole large bite into his mouth. Immediately Roland followed his lead, and Bonnie glanced up for her mother's disapproval. Instead, she got the biggest surprise of the evening, for her own proper mother was smiling warmly and enjoying the efforts of her younger children to pick up this new eating method.

Later, when Roland had thanked them and gone home, Bonnie heard her mother compliment her dad on his social sensitivity. She was bewildered only for a moment: her father's reply taught her a lifetime's lessons in graciousness. He said, "There's nothing more to good manners than making the other fellow feel comfortable."

Isn't that the heart of the matter, after all? Courtesy is not something that goes in and out of style. It is timeless. It is not so much what you do or say as it is your genuine interest in making life easier and more pleasant for those around you. It boils down to recognizing the worth and feelings of every human being you meet each day. Courtesy is the humble hourly practice of Christian love and interest for others.

Edmund Burke said: "Manners are of more importance than laws. Upon them in a great measure, the laws depend. The law touches us but here and there, and now and then. Manners are what vex or soothe, corrupt or purify, exalt or debase, barbarize or refine us, by a constant, steady, uniform, insensible operation, like that of the air we breathe." (*Richard Evans' Quote Book*, p. 169.)

Let us not in haste or ignorance forget our best manners. Let us not forget to respect the importance of each person around us, whether we will never see him again or whether we live with him constantly. May we each develop a gracious heart.

Stop, Look, and Listen

You know the children's song about the train barreling down the track, and you've heard young voices enthusiastically sing its warning; but have you ever really thought about these words? "Stop, look, and listen." There's an important message for us there.

Do you ever feel as if the hustle and hassle of each day gathers you up and propels you into the next day? Do details become more important than concepts? Do you get so involved in the moment's task that you forget that the task is just a part of a project and that the project has a long-term purpose?

It's easy to do. We can go months without doing anything really meaningful to us. We often leave last year's goals unmet because we just don't seem to get around to them. Soon that year is gone — and with it may go a friend, a child, an opportunity that we were too busy for.

Sometimes we let our busyness carry us away until we become like the idols David wrote about: "Eyes have they, but they see not: they have ears but they hear not." (Psalm 115:5-6.) We need to stop, look and listen.

Failure to keep our priorities in order and to pay attention to the things we value most, *making* time for them, can result in our losing them. That can be nothing but sad and painful — perhaps even tragic.

I guess the prime example of the important item that gets pushed aside or taken for granted is the family. A song lyric says, "I get so busy I forget I'm in love with you." Think about that. What if on your judgment day the Lord asked you where your spouse was and you could answer only, "I forgot"?

And what about your children? They grow each year into new people. If you want to know the pleasures of your five-year-old, *this* is the year—next year he'll be replaced by a six-year-old, and six is quite a different story.

When that little hand tugs at your sleeve and the tiny voice says, "Can we go swing?" go! Go then while the voice is asking, and learn the sheer joy of sunshine and breeze in your hair; hear the music of that child's laughter while it still rings. When the ten-year-old brings a book to read to you or a model to build, *then* is the time to set aside whatever keeps you busy and share what might keep you learning and growing and building relationships. When a child asks you to "come and see," that is the moment to stop and look. When your teenager is ready to tell you all the long details of his day, that is the time to listen. If you stop, look, and listen when your child first needs you, he will come to you again later. If you don't, you may join the parents who complain: "My kids never talk to me; they never join the rest of us to do anything together. Our family is falling apart!"

The same principle applies in all facets of our lives. Personal relationships with friends, co-workers, in-laws, and neighbors are all built on making time and paying attention. So are successes in business, sports, hobbies, budgets, school, and church. All we need to do is evaluate (What is *really* important? Which direction do I want to go? Do I need to make a change?) and then *act on that evaluation*, not on the pressure of an immediate but unimportant fuss. Certainly we want to see that TV program, wash the car, dust the living room, clean off the desk, retype the report; but we need to stop and ask *why*. If *any* activity, however worthy, fills up time we could be spending on progress toward our personal goals, it should be scrapped. It is not enough to be busy; we need to be productive, we need to give our best time and effort to our best goals.

Let me remind you of a great principle taught by Jesus Christ and recorded by Luke. You'll remember that on this occasion the Savior was instructing the multitude on what they must do to become his disciples. It boils down to setting priorities and not letting anything get in the way of our most important goals. His point is that we cannot leave it to chance — we ourselves must slam on the brakes and look about us to see that we are on the right track and then plan how to proceed.

"For which of you, intending to build a tower, sitteth not down first, and counteth the cost, whether he have sufficient to finish it?

"Lest haply, after he hath laid the foundation, and is not able to finish it, all that behold it begin to mock him,

"Saying, This man began to build, and was not able to finish.

"Or what king, going to make war against another king, sitteth not down first, and consulteth whether he be able with ten thousand to meet him that cometh against him with twenty thousand?

"Or else, while the other is yet a great way off, he sendeth an ambassage, and desireth conditions of peace.

"So likewise, whosoever he be of you that forsaketh not all that he hath, he cannot be my disciple." (Luke 14:28-33.)

It seems to me that as we strive to become his disciples, we need to stop our hurrying about, to look at ourselves, to listen to his counsel. If we'll take time to do that, then we'll also be more apt to stop, look, and listen to those who really count: husbands and wives, children and parents, brothers and sisters and friends. As we do that, perhaps (as the Savior says) we will discover that there are some things we need to forsake. Life isn't necessarily more meaningful the fuller we pack it. Sometimes we hurry so fast we lose it all.

May I give you my witness that this is a great principle. When I last heard that children's song, I heard more than children's voices — I heard the truth. In each life there is need to pause in the daily rush for planning and assessment. We need to stop, look, and listen in order to prepare for the challenges ahead and to receive the fullest measure of each day's experience as it comes. This is the way to fuller living.

Keeping Christmas

How are you keeping Christmas this year? In the same old way you've kept it every year? It seems that traditions are particularly important at this time of year. We fall comfortably into a pattern of preparation — a pattern of decorating, sharing wishes, baking, caroling, making lists, shopping, practicing for programs, watching for sales, wrapping gifts, sending cards, hurrying, waiting in lines, running out of money, fighting crowds, rewriting lists, worrying about details, mailing packages, smiling through dull parties, battling the traffic, over-eating, seldom sleeping, rushing, buying, getting, going. The pattern accelerates, doesn't it? And the speed is dizzying, making our heads spin until we cannot see beyond the moment's frenzy to that quiet and joyfully holy spirit of Christmas that we all somehow remember but can't seem to recapture.

Isn't that ironic? The celebration of mankind's ultimate triumph, the birth of the Savior, is marked by a celebration of *things*. No matter what our intentions are, we tend to rank goods and tasks above people during Christmas season. Mother has to run to get the shopping done so she can come home and decorate the house. Then, when she is in the middle of creating special holiday goodies for a party, her kids hover around her with questions and chatter and school books and friends and socks to mend and hair to braid and requests for a ride to the mall. "Enough is enough," she shouts at them, and sends them away offended.

And father, under pressure to be Santa Claus, puts in extra hours at work and begins to agonize over the additional bills. Year-end taxes loom only a few weeks past the holidays, and records, inventories, and a multitude of details demand attention at this season in almost any job. Dad has to plan on pulling the year together at its close, and in the meantime there's snow to shovel and awful traffic to contend with and a certain amount of shopping he just can't avoid. Then the family expects him to keep lending them ten-dollar bills and decorate the tree and entertain friends. Finally he becomes sullen and withdrawn; he blocks it all out and gets wrapped up in TV football.

See how all that "Christmas cheer" turns dismal? We get so involved in the things we do at Christmas that we forget about the people we're doing them for. We let the pressure mount until it makes us crabby and drives us apart, and then we feel disappointed about the spirit that's missing. And all the gifts and celebrating in the world won't make up for that disappointment. Can you remember, after all, what everybody gave you last year, or the year before, or in 1967? Things don't matter nearly as much as we think they do when we're scrambling to buy them; tasks don't matter as much as we think they do when we're trying to finish them. People matter. The people in your home and at your job and around your block — even the people who clerk in the stores you rush through and those you pass on the crowded December streets — the *people* matter. The warmth and hope and brotherhood we can share matter, and we share them more by little gestures than by grand gifts.

This kind of spirit is reflected in a letter to the editor of the *Deseret News* published January 5, 1977. The writer, Evalyn Bennett, found real Christmas right in the midst of one of those holiday hassles that can fray the nerves. She found it there because she found people supporting one another there. She wrote:

"I caught the real spirit of Christmas at the post office. In that hectic, over-crowded lobby, a concern for total strangers by total strangers was displayed a dozen times during my hour's wait. Christmas chemistry was working like magic, and everyone felt it. An elderly woman, obviously not well, was leaning against the wall waiting for someone who was mailing a package. A man at the end of the line stepped out and improvised a comfortable seat from a sturdy stand and a telephone book. The woman sank to her perch nodding gratefully.

"A two-year-old was crying as he was being held by his distraught mother. One grandmotherly woman found a box of crackers in a shopping bag, another woman found a key ring to delight the child.

"A man staggered under the load of about fifteen packages. He piled them on the floor with the help of those standing near him. It was a community effort to move the piles along the floor as the line moved forward, and there were more hands than were needed to lift the boxes to the counter when his turn came.

"An oriental teenager came in, and before long he was telling the woman next to him that this was his first Christmas and how excited he was about it. Everyone within earshot wanted to know more and shouted questions and greetings to him.

"A woman with her arms full of bundles set her young daughter on the desk so the waiting would be easier for both of them. Not a person passed the little girl without a tickle, a question, a comment or a candy bar. The little girl glowed from all the attention.

"A woman stooped with age got to the window and found she needed more staples in her mailing folder. An accommodating employee brought her a stapler, saving her a trip back home.

"Finally a tough-looking guy in a leather jacket came in and stood at the door watching the room full of people chattering and laughing. He said, 'This is something else. I come from a big city and believe me, I've never seen anything like this.' "

When the woman who wrote had reached the post office window and concluded her business there, the clerk smiled sincerely and said, "Have a really good day." "Thank you," she answered, "I already have!"

How little it takes to make a good day or a happy season! It's really easy to lift your eyes from the floor, to smile, to relinquish your grip on the thousand details that pressure you — if you remember that what's important are the souls around you. What greater celebration would the Lord himself accept than our sharing of hope and strength with one another? Of all seasons, Christmas is the time to recognize the light in the eyes of those we meet, to see the humanity we have in common, to acknowledge the look that says: "I'm human, too; I face what you face. I, too, am caught up in the joys and the anguish of life."

Can you keep Christmas this year? Can you create and maintain that happy, holy spirit that binds people together and buoys them up? Henry Van Dyke suggested how. He wrote:

"Are you willing to forget what you have done for other people, and to remember what other people have done for you; to ignore what the world owes you, and to think what you owe to the world; to put your rights in the background, and your duties in the middle distance, and your chances to do a little more than your duty in the foreground; to see that your fellowmen are just as real as you are; and try to look behind their faces to their hearts, hungry for joy; to own that probably the only good reason for your existence is not what you are going to get out of life, but what you are going to give to life; to close your book of complaints against the management of the universe, and look around you for a place where you can sow a few seeds of happiness — are you willing to do these things even for a day? Then you can keep Christmas.

"Are you willing to stoop down and consider the needs and the desires of little children; to remember the weakness and loneliness of people who are growing old; to stop asking how much your friends love you, and ask yourself whether you love them enough; to bear in mind the things that other people have to bear on their hearts; to try to understand what those who live in the same house with you really want, without waiting for them to tell you; to trim your lamp so that it will give more light and less smoke, and to carry it in front so that your shadow will fall behind you; to make a grave for your ugly thoughts and a garden for your kindly feelings, with the gate open — are you willing to do these things even for a day? Then you can keep Christmas.

"Are you willing to believe that love is the strongest thing in the world — stronger than hate, stronger than evil, stronger than death — and that the blessed life which began in Bethlehem nineteen hundred years ago is the image and brightness of the Eternal Love? Then you can keep Christmas.

"And if you keep it for a day, why not always?

"But you can never keep it alone."

It's true: we cannot keep Christmas alone. There is not enough tinsel in the world to brighten the self-centered heart. Not one of us can keep Christmas by getting; by pushing, wrapping, buying; by hurrying, preparing, worrying. We can keep Christmas only by raising our eyes to meet those of our fellow men and thus sharing the light of Christ. May we make an effort to truly keep Christmas every day of every year!

Have a Loving Time

A first-grade school teacher began the year with some different plans than her colleagues had. She was going to do away with show-and-tell. After her announcement to the class about her plans, a shy, curly-haired girl named Teresa approached her desk.

"Teacher," she said, "instead of show-and-tell, can we have a loving time?"

The teacher was not quite sure what she meant, so she asked Teresa to explain. This was the unforgettable answer. Teresa said: "Every once in a while you could lift us and give us a hug, and we could tell you something important. It wouldn't take long."

So from that day on, whenever a child needed a loving, he would stand close to the teacher's desk and receive a hug, a pat, and a few moments of the teacher's undivided attention while he told her something "important."(Marguerite J. Booth, *The Instructor*, November 1968.)

Just like Teresa in this first-grade class, we all have a crying need to be loved. We need to feel important to somebody. We have to feel that even when we're in our dirty working clothes, even if our hair is messed up by the breeze, even when we say the wrong thing or forget our friend's birthday, we are still loved.

Anyone who has ever had house plants knows that they simply must be watered. Who can count the number of Boston ferns that have perished because somebody neglected them? Oh, it's a gradual process. A plant doesn't die all at once. It turns from a healthy, vibrant green to a sickly yellow-green. One leaf and then another falls off and then it's gone. No water, no plant.

People are the same: they perish without love. Oh, it may not be readily apparent, but there is a gradual withering away of the spirit. Little by little life loses its joy and meaning. Without love, only the shell of a person remains.

Examine your own motivation in life. Why do you do most of the things you do every day? Think about it. It's mostly to be loved and admired by all you know. You want to be a somebody.

One family had two little girls and, as fate would have it, one of the girls had the curliest hair and the other had hair that was straight as spaghetti. Of course, the straight-haired child envied her sister. Every night her dreams were filled with visions of masses and masses of curly hair. Finally the straight-haired child's grandmother noticed her feelings and took her to a beauty salon where a near miracle occurred. She had a permanent. When she came out of the salon, she too had curls. And as she walked down the street she kept saying to her grandmother: "Did you notice; did you see that? Everybody's looking at me; they think I'm so cute." The truck drivers that rolled down the street, the mailman — the child was sure that everyone, everyone was looking at her. What a feeling!

Two thousand years ago a little group of listeners surrounded our Savior and asked him which of the many commandments was the most important. "Which is the great commandment in the law?" they asked, and then leaned forward with great expectancy to hear his answer. The answer was a simple one, "Thou shalt love. . . ." (Matthew 22:36-37.)

Why is love the most important? It is probably the most important because it is the most powerful of any human ability. Who can resist the power of love? Sometimes I think that when we see the Lord again after our mortal journey he won't ask how many buildings we built or the number of clubs we joined. I think he'll simply ask us, "Did you learn to love your brothers and sisters?"

Do you want to hear about love at work? There was once an elderly woman staying in a certain convalescent home. She was not well and had not been for some time. She had pretty well given up: she just sat in her rocking chair all day long; she didn't rock herself, she didn't read or watch television. She hadn't even spoken to anyone for three years — not a single word!

Clearly, she wasn't much fun to take care of — she never responded at all to the nurses who fed her, dressed her, brought her medicine. They began to turn her care over to the newest or lowest-ranking staff member.

One young nurse who began work at the convalescent home and was assigned to help this aging patient decided that she would make a difference. She had always considered herself a Christian, and the thought occurred to her that her Christian love was only as good as her love for this silent old woman. She pulled up another rocking chair and sat with her patient, rocking quietly and loving her without making any demands. For hours this young nurse simply rocked alongside the old lady and loved her as best she could. On the third day the old woman opened her eyes and said, "You are so kind." Within two weeks she was out of the home.

There is the power of love: the ability to bring words out of a three-year silence, the strength to give hope and the will to recover to one who has given up. Human love shared openly can succeed where all our science and skill and technology fails.

Think how you yearn for admiration and support, for someone who thinks you're much better than you are; then give that same kind of love to somebody else. You can lift a life. Your love can work a miracle.

But I must share one secret with all those who would seek to obey this first and great commandment. You can never love mankind in general. No, love is specific in its action. It is one person reaching out to one other. It is one parent rocking a child when it's inconvenient to do so, one neighbor noticing that the widow needs her lawn mowed or walks shoveled, one man passing on a kind word to another for a job well done. Those who rest back in their easy chairs and believe they love everyone are about as effective as those who utter prayers that say, "Bless everybody," and never lift a finger to help.

Make today the day you worry less about being lovable and

more about being loving. Choose someone to bless with your attention. Help a friend walk a little taller for having seen you that day. Fulfill in someone that eternal yearning to be a somebody.

In terms of eternal life, the failure to share love is just as fatal as the failure to breathe. Look around. Someone needs you. Have the vision to see him and the heart to respond.

No Replacement for Mothers

Ours is a world of chaos. Public morals shift and slide, wars are waged and threatened, fuel and food are in short supply, governments fall, prices rise. We seem to be at the whim of leaders whom we don't quite trust and markets we can neither control nor understand. Still, we yearn for stability and peace. The great minds of this era strain to deal with crises and conundrums, to solve the insolvable, to wrench some kind of order out of what certainly appears to be uncontrollable flux.

Why? Why do we struggle for the apparently impossible goal of security and peace? We do so because it is in our nature. All men, no matter what their background or experience, no matter what their creed or situation, need love and a place to belong and some certainty as to their role and importance. Joseph Smith put it this way: "If there is anything virtuous, lovely, or of good report or praiseworthy, we seek after these things." (Articles of Faith 1:13.)

The irony of the situation is that for too many of us this frantic search goes on all around the solution. Those qualities of life and those human characteristics we need so desperately can be found in every solid home and in every true and loving mother.

That seems a little simplistic, I know; but if you give it some thought you will realize that nations do not exhibit warmth, tolerance, patience, self-sacrifice, or wisdom. People do. Mothers, of all people, do it best.

Perhaps the reason we fail to see good old mom as a world-shaping influence is that she plays her role not before the masses, not under lights with a microphone, not in public documents, not for the media, but privately for children who seldom number over half a dozen. Hers is the healing of one broken heart, the teaching of an innocent mind, the comforting of two tear-filled eyes. These humble, private offerings require the strength and wisdom, the love and the will, to offer up a human soul. A mother pours her whole being into her family, and it is there — in the family — that we see the pattern of security and solidarity that we want for the world.

Throughout history, the stabilizing influence not only in the home and community but also in nations has been rendered by women who served as mothers. Those nations who boast a people strong and self-disciplined, courageous and compassionate, are consistently those nations that have had healthy homes with mothers who transmitted to their children values of eternal worth. Perhaps one might even say that all the lofty ideas and transcendent purposes which are envisioned in the personality of man are a reflection of our experiences and our associations with mother.

Now, I want you to give some serious thought to this question: Who could replace your mother in your life? No matter how comfortable you may be with your friend, your doctor, your accountant, your teacher, your attorney, your grocer, your banker, your mechanic, you know you could find someone else to fill their roles if you had to. Could you find another to fill your own mother's role in your life?

Mothers shape the world by shaping its population, one at a time. They provide daily stability and comfort to the people of this world so subtly and so quietly that we seldom notice. How do they accomplish this? Elder Spencer W. Kimball gives this example:

"I was in a northwestern city for an evening missionary meeting. I had arrived early in the day on the only available flight. The stake president was a busy man and I said to him, 'You go on about your work. Just give me a table and your typewriter, and I have plenty of things to do all afternoon.'

"So I started to work. Two or three hours passed so rapidly that I hardly realized the time had flown, and it must have been about 3 P.M. when I heard the front door open. While the father was out at work, the mother was upstairs ironing and sewing. Now the front door opened a crack and a child's voice said: 'Oh, Mother!' I listened and heard the warm, loving voice from upstairs say, 'I'm up here, dear. Do you want something?'

" 'Nothing, Mother,' said the little boy, and he slammed the door and went out to play.

"In a few minutes the door opened again and another boy stepped in, and a little older voice called, 'Mother!' Again I heard the voice from upstairs say, 'Here I am, darling. Do you want something?'

" 'No,' was the reply, and the door closed again and another child went out to play.

"In a little while, there was still another voice, that of a fifteen-year-old girl. She came rushing in, quite surprised to find a stranger in the home. She too called, 'Oh, Mother!' And to this the response was again, 'I'm up here, darling. I'm ironing.' That seemed to satisfy this young girl completely, and she went about her piano practice.

"A little later there was a fourth voice, a seventeen-year-old girl voice. The call upstairs was repeated and the same mother voice responded and invited her to come up if she wanted to. But she just sat down at the living room table and spread out her books and began studying.

"Mother was home! That was the important thing! Here was security!" (*The Miracle of Forgiveness* [Bookcraft, 1969], pp. 254-255.)

I'm sure none of this is news — we all know the nature and depth of a mother's influence, and we all know how it is conveyed. But usually we fail to acknowledge it, much less demonstrate our understanding or appreciation of it. We may talk about wonderful motherhood, we may go all out on Mother's Day, we may choke up when we have to leave home; but what about all the days in between occasions or crises? A large part of what makes mother's influence so far-reaching is the fact that it is constant. Is our demonstrated thanks equally constant? Don't we assume that mother is always there, interested in whatever's on our minds? Don't we allow her endless and thankless work in the home to shackle her without giving thought to her as an individual who may have interests beyond laundry, and meals, and mending, and picking up after us, and countless other tasks? Don't we often make mental note of her sacrifices but fail to express that notice in our behaviors and attitudes?

No matter what we say, no matter how lofty our sentiments about mothers, if we don't laud and respect, support and cherish the mothers in our lives, if we fail to make consistent, active expression of our love, if we neglect to serve them in return, then we send the women who serve as mothers a clear message: you don't matter to me; your interests aren't important; you exist only to wait on me. Thus we help fuel the fire that is sending women from their homes looking for a place where they will be valued and appreciated.

Let us not let that happen. Let us understand that if people last an eternity but buildings last five hundred years, it is more important to raise children than buildings. Let us really act on the truth that a child has the potential to be like the Lord but today's best-seller will one day be just dust, and so it is more important to write poems on a child's soul than to write them in a book.

In a chaotic world it is motherhood that holds the strands of life together. And if home is a refuge of peace, it is because a mother has made it so.

As I Have Loved You...

See if you recognize yourself anywhere among these people: The parent who sacrifices his desires and needs, his time and effort, for a child who says, "You don't understand me. You don't care what I want." The friend who loyally stands by a person who complains, "I'm always alone in my struggles." The student who almost worshipfully strives to please a teacher who says accusingly, "I have feelings too, but the kids never notice — they just think I'm an automaton." The scoutmaster who encourages and praises a boy who remarks, "Nobody really cares what I do." The husband or wife who really tries to share with and support and comfort a spouse who says, "You don't really love me." Have you ever been there?

We all experience times when we just don't seem to be able to make that important person feel our love. Maybe he's not receptive, or perhaps we're not communicating well. It's possible that we don't know how to give love in the first place, no matter how loving we want to be. Whatever the cause, such times are frustrating and painful; for something deep in our souls affirms that to love and be loved affords life's greatest joys. If we just knew how to do it, we'd all be happier.

There is a simple guide to loving given by the Savior to his disciples at the Last Supper. Said he, "As I have loved you, . . . love one another." (John 13:34.) How shall we love? As Christ did. We can find that understanding, we can create and maintain that joyous interpersonal communion, if we give love in the same manner as the Lord gave love. With that in mind, it seems logical to look closely at those mortals whom he touched during his ministry and to learn from his example. May I suggest four principles that appear to delineate Christ's love.

First of all, Jesus did not choose the people he loved from those who could do something for him. He did not court the wealthy or the influential; he traveled among those who needed him — the sinners, the publicans, the poor, the ill. How easily we become selective — whether we intend to or not — about those who will see our best efforts! For the boss, for the bishop, for the rich old uncle, we put on our best behavior, we run the extra mile, we dress up. Sometimes our selectiveness reflects a sense of image-improvement: we choose friends who embody our goals, as if running with the rich or beautiful or witty could make us so too.

Remember the neighborhood clubhouse with the sign that said, "No girls [or no boys] allowed"? How does the adult version of the "in group" and the "out group" at work or at school or in the community differ in spirit from that childish restriction? At some point *you* will be the one "not allowed" in some groups, and that can be pretty painful unless you have determined in advance to include in your love those who can help you *and* those who cannot — or even will not. Remember Edwin Markham's famous verse:

> He drew a circle that shut me out —
> Heretic, rebel, a thing to flout;
> But love and I had the wit to win:
> We drew a circle that took him in.

The first identifying feature of Christ's love is that it is not exclusive. If we are to love as he did, we must extend our concern and regard to all — including those who can do nothing for us and those who perhaps have no regard for us. Recall that at the trial which led to his crucifixion Jesus had no powerful friend who could stand up for him. He had not showered his attention on men who could save him, and he bore no ill will for those who would not.

I like this image of nonrestrictive love: "When a wise man names his brothers, he draws no circle smaller than the first one ever drawn on the earth. In the beginning, God gave the world its shape. He made it round."

The second feature of Christ's love is that it was given without being asked for. Jesus did not say, "Let me know if I can help." He never waited to be told who needed him and for what; he observed life around him and filled unspoken needs. Do you recall the man who was waiting at the pool called Bethesda for a chance to be cleansed of his thirty-eight-year infirmity? He was alone there and apparently so ill that he could not move; for when the Lord saw him and spoke to him asking if his desire was to be made whole, the man replied that he had no one to help him into the pool and that when he tried to get to it himself others stepped in front of him. Here was an individual who was pretty generally ignored and who lay quietly near the pool bearing his troubles patiently. Jesus did not wait for him to speak, nor did he assume the man's silence meant he needed no help. Rather, Jesus sought this man in conversation and healed him then and there. (See John 5:2-8.)

This is no isolated occurrence. The scriptures are full of Jesus' sensitivity to the needs of those he encountered. He required no invitation to serve, no acknowledgment, no request; he attended all who needed him, whether or not they had courage to ask for him. If we are to love as Christ loved, we must learn to sense and respond spontaneously to need.

A third quality of the Savior's love is tender attention to people and feelings before things and events. By putting a man's or woman's heart first, Christ said to that person: "You are important. You matter." That is the kind of affirmation we need if we are to believe we really are loved.

It is easy to get involved in life's business, to focus attention on the tasks or objects that fill our days. And in that preoccupation with accomplishing the job at hand, we too often neglect the people at hand. The father whose object is to plant a vegetable garden and who sends away his five-year-old's "helping hands" because they leave crooked rows and puddled mud and floating seeds is guilty of just such preoccupation. So is the brother who consistently closes his siblings out of his room, and the mother who cannot tolerate finger-prints *anywhere*. If we condemn another's effort to help or his interest in us or his fingerprints (however large or small), we condemn *him* by saying his intentions do not count. Love and condemnation cannot survive together.

Near the end of his ministry, Jesus was visiting in the house of Mary and Martha. Mary brought expensive oil to anoint his feet as a gesture of love. Certainly the Lord did not require this, and the suggestion was made that such costly oil might be more profitably used to advance the Lord's work if it were sold and the money given to the poor. However valid the idea might have been, Jesus considered first the woman before him and her feelings, and he would allow no one to criticize her gesture. To love as Christ loved, we must place our fellow beings above material goods, above momentary concerns, above convenience and expediency.

The fourth principle of Christ's manner of loving is that he loved mankind in particular, not in general. It doesn't require much to "love everybody" or to pray, "Please bless all the world"; but it's quite a different matter to give love to one person or to serve a single human being and thereby bless the world yourself.

Jesus loved and served individual persons, not the populace at large. He blessed the children one by one; he healed each person of his own particular infirmity. When he met the woman of Samaria at the well, he knew her — her past, her needs, her living arrangements, her sorrows. He spoke to her personally, not as another face in the crowd. To love as Christ loved, we have to reach out to individuals and not content ourselves with vague feelings of general goodwill. Love extends from one heart to another single heart; it is risky and rewarding to give because it *does* involve us with another soul whose needs and feelings we cannot control. To experience shared loved as Jesus did, we must make that personal and individual offering of our feelings to and for another.

"As I have loved you" — freely, openly, individually, sensitively, without selectivity — "love one another." This was given to the disciples as a commandment, and it applies to us as well. Our practice of Christian love is the means for the Lord to bless all his children. We must not neglect it.

Among the rubble left in one heavily bombed European city after the war, a church congregation found a statue of Christ. It was pretty battered, and the hands had been broken off; but the people had always valued it and could not bear to part with it. They debated as to a way to restore it and investigated craftsmen who might be able to repair it.

Their final solution creates an image and reminder for all of us: the statue remains as it was found after the war, but next to it stands a sign which reads, "We are the hands of Christ."

We too can become the hands of Christ, by learning to love as he loved.

Just Be Nice

A father, trying to counsel his teenaged children to be more positive in their responses to those they met, found himself getting nowhere. His admonitions to "be civil," "stay calm," "try to think before speaking," and "smile occasionally" were met with blank stares.

Finally, in exasperation, he exclaimed, "For Pete's sake, just learn to be *nice!*" Now, that's pretty good advice, spoken simply and directly.

I'm sure you have read or heard this suggestion: "Whatever you do, keep smiling — it makes people wonder what you've been up to!" I suppose the reason we find that amusing is that it's true, but isn't it also kind of sad that it *is* true? If we *do* suspect the person with a smile on his face, what does that say about us?

Think for just a minute about the last time you made a kind gesture just because you felt like it. That smile, that cheerful word, that extra minute to listen to a friend, was well worth the small effort it cost you, wasn't it? And if the person who received that gesture suspected you of being up to something, would it have been his fault for doubting or would it have been *your* fault for not making such gestures more often?

We all know people who are generally nice, who radiate kindness and goodwill most of the time. We do not doubt their motives. As a matter of fact, these are the people whom we trust and whose company we seek. Their nice gestures are the indications of their nature — they really *are* nice.

"Well, good for them," we may think. "It's easy to *act* nice if you *are* nice." But I suggest to you that the principle works just as easily in the opposite direction. If you practice giving the kind and generous deed or word, before long it will seem natural to you and soon it will indeed become your nature. As a bonus, you'll find that everyone you meet will help you by responding in kind, and soon most people will seem to be more pleasant because — at least with you — they too will begin practicing.

All that sounds almost too optimistic, but there is scientific evidence to support the relationship between how we act and how we are, and to underscore the power of kindness and response. Let me share with you the story of an experiment in kindness as it was told to me by my friend Reed Bradford at Brigham Young University.

"Several years ago a friendly, lovable little puppy appeared at one of the buildings of the Kellogg Sanitarium in Battle Creek, Michigan. At once, some of the staff members opened their hearts to him and treated him with all possible kindness. He wagged his tail with such enthusiasm that his whole little body wagged along with it. He was the happiest pup that any of the staff had ever seen. Any small thing they did for him made him wiggle in happy response.

"His very exuberance was responsible for an experiment that staff members decided to try. They took the pup into the operating room, administered an anesthetic, and made an incision in one of his legs. The purpose was to examine the marrow in his bones, which they found was a healthy pink, filled with red corpuscles. When the wound was carefully bound up, it healed rapidly.

"Then the word was passed around that no one was to smile at the pup or speak in a kind tone of voice to him for a period of six weeks. His keepers fed him just as they always had, but nobody petted him or showed any evidence of affection. Soon the poor little creature began to wilt visibly, and he became the most forlorn little dog imaginable. He crept disconsolately into the dark corners and his tail dragged along the floor.

"At the conclusion of the six-week period the little puppy was taken back into the operating room and the marrow of the same bone was re-examined. This time it was a brownish, unhealthy color, and red corpuscles were very scarce. The wound required a long time to heal despite the fact that, once again, staff members began to shower all their positive emotions on the little puppy. He responded very slowly to their overtures, and it was a long time before he wagged his tail again. Something vital had gone out of him when kindness was denied him.

"When at last the little dog's enthusiasm for life had been fully restored, when he wagged his tail briskly and seemed to smile at everyone, he was taken once more to the operating room where the marrow in the bone was found to be pink and beautiful again."

I suppose the logical conclusion to that story is that without kindness it's a dog's life. Or at least it's a sad dog's life.

If being nice has such a profound effect on animals — on their physical as well as behavioral condition — what tremendous power it must have on humans! It is not unrealistic to conclude that the practice of kindness can change an individual life and could perhaps affect a much larger community.

The Primary children sing this verse:

> I want to be kind to ev'ryone,
> For that is right, you see.
> So I say to myself: "Remember this,
> Kindness begins with me."
> ("Kindness Begins with Me," *Sing with Me*, B-49.)

That's where it starts — with the individual — with you, with me. And when it starts is now, today, at our jobs, in our homes. It requires some discipline and self-control to begin with, but it can be done.

Think how much nicer home would be if parents disciplined with kindness, remembering that children deserve "please" and "thank you" too. Imagine what a joy it would be if kids answered their parents cheerfully and tried to be pleasant about doing their parts at home. Extend that image into your job, your school, your community. Such simple practices as smiling, controlling a temper, offering a compliment, speaking politely, and listening courteously could affect the whole world for better if enough people began to exercise them consistently.

Even if changing the entire world isn't your goal, being nice is worthwhile for the change it can bring about in *your* world. Each of us in striving to improve should keep in mind this example: "Turn unto the Lord your God: for he is gracious and merciful, slow to anger, and of great kindness." (Joel 2:13.)

It really doesn't matter whether you are rewarded or praised for being kind—the improvement it can bring within your own life is enough. Cicero's words, now two thousand years old, are still true: "If we lose affection and kindliness from our life, we lose all that gives it charm."

May we redouble our resolve to pay attention to the small but important gestures of goodwill that can improve our enjoyment of one another and increase our development of Christian traits. May we learn to be kind by adopting a kind manner, and may we practice in the common moments of our lives.

The Little Things

Television occasionally has a special or a movie billed as "The Big Event." Detergents come in boxes labeled "giant" or "colossal" or "king size." In our society we're pretty thoroughly conditioned to believe that bigger is better. But in spite of all the advertisers' "big" talk, I believe the world really belongs to little things. It was, after all, a single straw that broke the camel's back. And you know yourself that it's the paper clip you can't find or the one button that's missing or the little bill you didn't expect that sends you into a tailspin.

Do you know how tiny a virus is? If you lined up a thousand average-sized human cells end to end, they might extend half an inch. Inside each one of those cells you could put over sixty million polio viruses. That's what I call *small*. Yet that minuscule virus and other kinds of viruses just as tiny cause half the world's diseases.

Here's another little thing that has to do with your health. Have you ever heard of Ignaz Semmelweis? He got concerned about the very high number of women who died of a terrible fever after giving birth in Vienna hospitals during the early nineteenth century. He investigated and found that many doctors went to deliver babies directly after dissecting cadavers, so he ordered all attendants to wash their hands in chlorinated water before deliveries. That one little thing — hand washing — saved hundreds of lives within the next year and drew attention to a principle that has affected medicine ever since.

You wonder if little details can really be all that important? Try not putting oil in your car for a year and see what happens to your engine. A single gunshot will start an avalanche of thousands of tons of mountain snow, snapping trees like twigs and burying everything in its path. And, of course, it was partly a quest for so small an item as spice to cook with that sent Columbus on the voyage that revealed the New World to Europe.

The same principle applies in human relationships — it's the little gestures we make for others that really show our love. Said Lord Chesterfield, "Trifles, little attentions, mere nothings either done or neglected will make you either liked or disliked in the general run of the world."

Christ's great commandment to us seems easy enough to follow: "love one another; as I have loved you." (John 13:34.) We know that we'd do anything to help a friend or neighbor in trouble. If his house burned or he lost his job or got very ill and was in the hospital, we'd be right there to help. But life isn't sufficiently full of crises to justify our waiting around for dramatic, earthshaking events to show our love. People need us every day in simple, quiet ways — they don't wear signs that say "Treat me gently" or "I need praise today." We have to be wise enough to see those needs and to fill them just as quietly as they are expressed.

Marriage is a prime example of a relationship in which people need one another's very special attention for daily support. When was the last time you left a love note on your mate's pillow? surprised her with some flowers for no reason at all? brought him hot cookies while he was writing checks to pay the bills? warmed up the car on a cold morning so the other wouldn't be uncomfortable the first few minutes? made the effort to look your best? noticed unsaid feelings and gave a word of encouragement? All little things — but it is just such little acts, remembered or forgotten, that have tremendous impact on the human heart.

W. E. Petersen tells a story about a little thing that made a lasting memory in the lives of three boys. It seems that during the waning years of the Depression, in a small southeastern Idaho community, a Mr. Miller had a roadside stand where he sold farm-fresh produce as the season made it available. Food and money were still extremely scarce, so barter and trade were often used.

Now, it seems that among the most frequent visitors to this roadside stand were three ragged but clean little boys who used to eye the produce with hungry, longing looks. The typical conversation between Mr. Miller and one of the boys went something like this:

"Hello, Barry, how are you today?"

"H'lo, Mr. Miller. Fine, thank ya. Jus' admirin' them peas — sure look good."

"They are good, Barry. Anthing I can help you with?"

"No, sir, jus' admirin' them peas."

"Would you like to take some home?"

"No, sir, got nuthin' to pay for 'em with."

"Well, what have you to trade with me for some of those peas?"

"All I got's my prize aggie — best marble around here."

At that, Miller would examine the marble carefully and say: "This marble's a dandy, all right. Only thing is, this one is blue. I sort of go for red. Do you have a red one like this at home?"

"Not 'zackly," the little boy would say, "but almost."

"Tell you what," Mr. Miller would answer. "Take this sack of peas home with you and next trip this way let me look at that red marble."

This bartering process went on with all three boys. When they came back with their red marbles — as they always would — Mr. Miller would change his mind, deciding he didn't like red after all. He would then send them home with a bag of produce for a green marble or perhaps an orange one.

Years passed, and the three ragged boys grew up to make their own way in the world. Then word came to each of them that Mr. Miller had died. All three came their distances to greet Mrs. Miller at the mortuary and offer whatever words of comfort they could find. Each of the young men hugged her, kissed her on the cheek, spoke briefly with her, and then moved on to the casket. Her misty, light blue eyes followed them as, one by one, each young man stopped briefly, placed his own warm hand over the cold, pale hand in the casket, and left the mortuary awkwardly wiping his eyes.

The next person in line got the whole story. It seems that all three young men had told her how much they had appreciated the things Jim Miller had "traded" them. Now, at last, when Jim could not change his mind about color or size, they had come to pay their debt. "We've never had a great deal of wealth of this world," she confided, "but right now Jim would consider himself the richest man in Idaho."

With loving gentleness Mrs. Miller lifted the lifeless fingers of her husband to reveal three magnificent, shiny red marbles lying there. (Retold from W. E. Petersen's "Three Marbles," *Ensign,* October 1975, p. 39.)

Now isn't that a little thing to remember your whole life—a few bags of peas or tomatoes given to a hungry boy? But that's the way of it. Little things rule the world—they always have and they always will.

Wisdom

Part 3

The Best Things in Life Aren't Free

Many of us know the old song that says, "The best things in life are free." Nice old song. But, you know, I think it's all wrong. Nothing is really free — and the best things are the most costly. Only sometimes they cost us more dearly than we could pay with dollars.

Does that sound surprising to you? Think about things that used to be free. Service at the gas station, for example. There was a time when you could buy a tank of gas and expect to have the oil checked, the tires checked, the windows washed, and the floor vacuumed — all free. If you asked, road maps were free too. Today you can get all those services, but you pay for them — in addition to the outrageous price of gasoline.

"What about nature?" you ask. "Sunsets are free. First frost is free." Well, here's where that more-than-dollars kind of cost comes in. I once heard a woman exclaim to her friend about a brilliant sunset, only to have the friend respond: "Oh, you're just like my husband, going on about a silly sunset. What's the big deal? The sun goes down. It happens every day — and it just means you have to drive in the dark!"

Now, no amount of money could have bought for that lady the soul-filling satisfaction of that sunset, and she was unwilling or unable to give what her friend and her husband gave for it: time and attention and appreciation. She reminded me of the Easterner my grandfather used to tell about. The man and his wife had driven all the way across the country to see the Grand Canyon. When they arrived, the man parked the car, got out and, before his wife could catch up with him, strode to the rim. "Yep!" he said, looking over the scene, "that's it. Let's go!"

All of us want to get more out of life, but too many are not willing to *give* more — to try harder, to invest our talents, our efforts, our hearts. Nobody is "just lucky." Those who get what they desire pay for it — one way or another. People ultimately get out of life in measures of success and joy exactly what they put into it. Another song lyric, this one from *The Sound of Music*, sums it up: "Nothing comes from nothing; nothing ever could." The greater the effort, the greater the reward. It's a simple formula.

You know, it wasn't the Goths that defeated Rome — it was the free circuses, or so historians believe. The once-tough Roman people softened up with their daily doses of indolence, power, and self-indulgence. To stay popular, their emperors gave them more and more of what they craved — the easy life. So in the year 410, when the hard-working and tough barbarians swept down upon Rome, they brought destruction to the greatest nation the world had ever seen. It was easy prey because its people believed in the easy life. They really believed they could get something for nothing. They wanted more and more for less and less — a philosophy that always has, in the end, a very high price.

You know who Frederick Loewe is — the Viennese composer who, with Alan Jay Lerner wrote the musical *My Fair Lady*. Loewe arrived in this country during the Great Depression when jobs were scarce at best, and jobs for musicians — even very gifted ones — were nonexistent. Short on money, Loewe fell behind on the payments for his piano, and the bank served notice to repossess it. On the morning the movers were to come for the instrument that was his joy as well as his means for living, Loewe sat at the keyboard to play for the last time. With a heavy heart he began lovingly fitting chords and tunes together and before long he was totally absorbed in his music. He did not hear or notice when the three movers arrived, so he was startled when he finished playing to look up and see them seated on his floor, listening intently. Without a word the three men rose and dug through their pockets until among them they came up with the overdue payment. They left the money on Loewe's piano and walked out empty-handed.

Was that charity? Hardly. Loewe saved his own piano by the way he played it — and that had cost him hours of practice, countless lessons, the development of talent, and a world of devotion. No half-hearted piano-pounder could have so touched the hearts of those movers. And Loewe had paid in advance, never suspecting his investment would be returned in just such a manner.

Every scientific advance, every kind of progress mankind has ever made, has been due to those few who really understood that nothing in this world is free. Any accomplishment — especially any great accomplishment — takes monumental effort. It takes sacrifice, even when it seems there can be nothing left to give. It takes energy, even when all energy seems to be drained.

Do you know how Madame Curie came to isolate radium? It wasn't just a lucky discovery in an easy moment. She sifted through tons and tons of coal in a drafty old barn. People ridiculed her and called her efforts futile, until after years of work she finally achieved her goal — isolating radium. Did those who lauded her, do those who praise her still, have any concept of how long those coal-sifting hours must have been in a cold, cold barn?

What about the father whose child runs to meet him after work and grows up to adore and support him and make him proud? Is that devotion free? Is it the natural outgrowth of any parent-child relationship? Or did that dad just get lucky? Absolutely not. The parent who has the total love and trust of his child has earned that at tremendous cost. That parent has foregone some personal interest to spend time with his child, has stopped the angry word in his throat when it would have been easier to yell, has awakened in the night to attend to the child's needs when it would have been nicer to sleep.

"Nothing comes from nothing; nothing ever could." That is true in developing a talent, advancing a great idea, even in providing for ourselves. And it is true in our seeking of the Lord.

There are those who sit back and complain that the Lord has no interest in them, when the fact is that they have no interest in him.

They say in prayer, "Bless everyone," but have no desire to help their next-door neighbor. They say, "Help me to be more in tune with thee," and then go and see an immoral movie.

I read of one young girl who decided to ask the Lord to help her lose some weight. When she told her aunt she was praying to lose weight, the aunt wisely replied, "Maybe, this time, you'd better *fast* and pray."

The Lord himself has stated that we are responsible for giving if we expect to receive:

"There is a law, irrevocably decreed in heaven before the foundations of this world, upon which all blessings are predicated —

"And when we obtain any blessing from God, it is by obedience to that law upon which it is predicated." (D&C 130:20-21.)

Do you say you want to know the Lord, and then give him only two minutes a day in prayer — a prayer that is a carbon copy of the prayer you uttered yesterday? Do you tell him you want to be a great and noble servant of his, and then spend your hours just watching whatever happens to be on TV? The best thing in life is not free. The best thing in this life or in any other is knowing your Heavenly Father and serving him and being worthy at the end of this mortal life to hear him say to you: "Well done. You have run a mighty race."

Be obedient. Serve. Sacrifice so that you may receive the good gifts of life now and the greatest gift — of life eternal — in time to come. These things are not free — they are costly. And they are worth it.

The Faith to Find Him

A man in Pennsylvania who was a farmer became bored with his trade. "There must be something more to life than this," he said, and he decided to try to sell his farm. He then wrote to his cousin in Canada and asked for employment in the coal oil business.

The cousin wrote back and said, "I'd like to hire you, but you don't know enough about coal oil."

"I'll fix that," said the farmer. That very day he began an industrious study into the whole field of coal oil. He wasn't going to let ignorance hold him back from his chosen career. He began his study clear back at the second day of God's creation. He learned all about the different stages of the earth's formation and discovered that giant forests had once covered the earth. Then, it seemed, the climate had grown colder and giant glaciers were formed, crushing the forests beneath their weight and leveling mountains and forming new rivers. The masses of vegetation had been buried, subjected to tremendous pressure, and eventually turned into beds of coal oil.

The farmer learned what coal oil looked like, what it smelled like; he knew its uses, its properties. At last, he decided, he was ready for his new employment in the coal oil business. He wrote his cousin and said he was leaving his farm behind forever. He was headed for a new career. He sold his farm for $833 and was on his way.

The new owner of the farm arrived and set about his work. One day, when he went out to water his cattle, he discovered a lovely stream for that purpose running behind the barn. Most curious about this stream, however, was a plank that the previous owner had placed edgewise across it and a kind of black muck that accumulated on the plank. The cattle would not stick their noses through the muck to get the water unless it was diverted. The new owner called the state geologists to examine the problem and find out just what the stuff was. He discovered that it was coal oil — a hundred million dollars' worth on that single farm! And the previous owner, who had believed himself an expert in coal oil, had sold his farm — his gold mine — for a mere $833. (From a story by Russell Conwell in the *New York Times*, November 1939.)

This incident is not unique. I know a college coed who got 100 percent on the written final in her golf class and still couldn't hit the ball. We all know a lot of things in theory that we just can't apply into our lives. We know how to be happy, rich, beautiful; but we are certainly not all happy, rich, and beautiful. We can expound for hours on the virtues of loving our neighbor, but we still edge somebody out of a parking spot if we get half a chance. We know a hundred ways to diet, but we're not skinny; we give ways to make a million in the stockmarket, but we're not millionaires. All of this is frustrating, surely, but it can also be dangerous. It can be dangerous because through it we may fool ourselves into believing we really understand something with our heart and soul that we know not at all. We may parrot knowledge that is really still beyond us.

The Lord knows this. He says that his people draw near him with their mouth and with their lips do honor him, but their hearts are far from him. (See Isaiah 29:13.) Many of us in the world think we really know the Lord. We can recite scriptures; we say our duty prayers; we earn gold stars on our foreheads for Sunday School attendance; and those things are certainly worthwhile, good things to do. But they alone do not mean we know the Lord. Activity does not mean that his friendship and fatherhood have really changed our lives, have lifted us above and beyond ourselves to commune with him. It does not mean the current of his love is flowing through our being, enlightening our every day. One of the world's great causes for sadness is the number of people who go through the motions of spirituality and are content with that alone, when the Lord offers so much more.

There is a difference between a settled, intellectual belief and the dynamic faith that is required in order to come unto the Lord. James wrote of this in a forceful epistle to the Saints of old. It seems some of them were resting comfortably, with the consciousness that they really believed in God, and that such belief was sufficient on their part. James reproved them thus: "Thou believest that there is one God; thou doest well: the devils also believe, and tremble." (James 2:19.)

In another New Testament instance an evil spirit had gained power over a man with such force as to control his actions and utterances. When he came into Christ's presence, however, his manner became pleading: "Let us alone," said the spirits, using his voice, "what have we to do with thee, thou Jesus of Nazareth? I know thee who thou art; the Holy One of God." (Luke 4:34.)

Has there ever been a more unreserved confession of belief than by these servants of Satan? Probably not. But their knowledge of Christ could not change their demonic state because they were wholly wicked and unwilling to be touched by him.

Compare the testimony of the demons with that of Peter when Christ asked him, "Whom say ye that I am?" Peter said with great emotion, "Thou art the Christ, the Son of the living God." (Matthew 16:15-16.) His words were perhaps not so different from those of the evil spirits, but in his hunger and thirst for righteousness he was eager to be touched and moved and vitalized by the Spirit of the Lord. Therein is the difference between a settled belief and a dynamic faith.

So, how well does each of us know the Lord? I've often pondered that when I've seen people reject religion, calling it inadequate. "I know all about that stuff," they say. "I've earned my Sunday School awards." I submit that very few of us have begun to experience the joy or fullness that can be ours when the Lord's Spirit really touches us, when we stop referring to mere routine as religion.

Why be an expert on coal oil if you're going to sell the farm that has a hundred million dollars' worth of it on the property? Are you selling yourself short too, thinking you have God in your pocket? Are you calling mechanical prayer, communion? Are you reading the scriptures, but never having one leap out at you with such force and clarity that its brilliance seems to burn into your soul? Are you fumbling through life, not ever hearing a voice that guides some people with such penetration that they're sure they've heard it somewhere before?

Make your faith a motivating force in your life. Yearn to be close to the Lord, and your strong desire will carry you to your goal.

Enlarge Your Soul

A certain farming community was facing a severe drought that threatened the farmers' crops and livelihood. Day after day, week after week, they looked for the precious rain, but nothing came. Finally, in desperation, they did what they should have done in the beginning—they decided to spend some time in fasting and prayer and then meet at their local church to supplicate the Lord for the much needed rain.

As they gathered there in church and prayed fervently for rain, it seems a miracle happened. They heard thunder, they saw the sky grow dark with clouds; and the heavens opened and poured rain upon the parched land. The service over, the people filed out of the church and started home in the downpour, grateful but drenched—all but one little girl, that is, who had planned ahead. As she left the church, she pulled out her umbrella and walked home protected from the rain. Among the hundreds gathered there, she was the only one who, in her simple childlike faith, had thought to bring an umbrella so as not to get wet.

In our modern world people tend to think of faith as a characteristic of the childish, the mindless, the puny. Many seem to think that the skeptic is the more intelligent, the more mature, the realistic. But is it really so? The scriptures give us a penetrating answer to that. Jesus said: "If ye have faith as a grain of mustard seed, ye shall say unto this mountain, Remove hence to yonder place; and it shall remove; and nothing shall be impossible unto you." (Matthew 17:20.) Ponder that. *Nothing* shall be impossible to you.

And again we read in Mark that Jesus said, "If thou canst believe, all things are possible to him that believeth." (Mark 9:23.) All things are possible to him that believeth. That is an amazing promise to those of us who live in a world where we sometimes feel increasingly helpless and powerless. The prophet Daniel used faith to stop the very jaws of the lions who would devour him; Moses used faith to part the Red Sea in defiance of the more obvious laws of nature. Faith, it seems, is a principle of power greater than any nuclear energy or any force yet untamed by man. Yet so few of us understand it, and so few of us really have learned to tap it for the life-giving sweetness it can add to our lives.

What is faith really, then? It is the assurance which men and women have of the existence of things which they have not seen. I have not seen tomorrow's sunrise, yet I have an assurance that it will take place. In fact, I am basing all my plans and activities around my faith in tomorrow's sunrise. Faith, in fact, is the moving cause of all action. Ask yourself what principle it is that excites you to any action, whether it be to start a new diet, to begin a new pursuit, to build a new home. Isn't it the belief you have in the existence of something that you have not seen? As a modern prophet said: "Would you exert yourselves to obtain wisdom and intelligence, unless you did believe that you could obtain them? Would you have ever sown, if you had not believed that you would reap? . . . Would you have ever asked, unless you had believed that you would receive? . . . In a word, is there anything that you would have done, either physical or mental, if you had not previously believed? Are not all your exertions of every kind, dependent on your faith?" (*A Compilation Containing the Lectures on Faith, etc.*, N. B. Lundwall, compiler, p. 8.)

The answer to that is clearly yes. We base our lives on the assurance of many things which we have not seen. And our faith is usually only as strong as our evidence. Without evidence, the mind cannot have faith in anything. Let me explain. I have faith that tomorrow the sun will rise because the sun has risen every day of my life. I can remember no morning in which the sun didn't rise. Oh, it may have been hidden by the clouds some days; but even when I couldn't see it, I still had evidence that it was there—the sky and earth grew light, the temperature rose. Even on cloudy days I had plenty of evidence of the existence of the sun which I could not see. Evidence of one kind or another precedes faith.

Once a proud grandmother was bragging to me about her new grandchild, a baby only four months old. She started to tell me how the baby talked, saying, "Mama," and "Daddy," and all sorts of words. I have to admit that I did not have much faith in her story. Why? Because all the evidence I had gathered through my life about babies led me to believe that four-month-old infants do not talk. I had never heard a four-month-old talk. I had never read of so small a child talking. I had no faith in what she said because I had no evidence to support it and plenty to deny it.

Our faith is usually strong or weak on a given matter according to the strength or the weakness of the evidence we have. Sometimes, in fact, we may misinterpret or misunderstand evidence and come to an entirely false faith. For centuries all of the inhabitants of the earth were deceived about the motion of the sun and the moon. They believed that all heavenly bodies revolved around the earth daily, based on their observations and their experience. When Copernicus came along and announced that the earth rotated, people were terribly upset. He presented a kind of evidence that shook their false faith. Many who followed Hitler during World War II were very zealous in their faith. They had taken someone's word as evidence that a master race existed, and they used their false faith to justify the killing of helpless people.

Now, a false faith in some areas may not be injurious to us as individuals or as nations. But a false understanding based on incorrect or incomplete evidence with regard to the existence of God and his plan for us can have most fearful consequences. Said Orson Pratt: "The faith of Paul, that Jesus of Nazareth was an imposter, led him to persecute his followers with great zeal. Afterwards his faith that Jesus was the son of God, led him to endure all kinds of hardships for his sake." (Lundwall, *Lectures on Faith*, p. 73.) So, what we have faith in, in this world really does make all the difference. We may be very zealous in our belief; but if the belief is not true, then all our efforts may have been in vain. Why work hard to scramble up a ladder if it is leaning against the wrong wall?

Well, then, in looking at the evidence we have that builds our faith, especially in regard to the purpose of this life, we must be very wise. We must understand that our traditions, our biases, our points of view, may make us misinterpret or misunderstand the evidence we have. But there is one sort of evidence that never fails. The formula was given us by an ancient prophet. He said that if we have just a desire to believe in the Lord and his love for us, even if we have no more than a particle of faith, we must plant it in our hearts and act upon it. And if we do, it will begin to swell.

"And when you feel these swelling motions, ye will begin to say within yourselves — It must needs be that this is a good seed, or that the word is good, for it beginneth to enlarge my soul; yea, it beginneth to enlighten my understanding, yea, it beginneth to be delicious to me." (Alma 32:28.)

Does your life's belief enlarge your soul? As you act upon what you believe, do you grow happier every day? That is the best evidence that your faith is a true one, based on true principles.

I know that the Lord lives. I have faith in his existence, faith granted to me by powerful evidence that I could never deny. I prize that faith; it governs my life. May all who read these words discover the power of true faith in their lives also.

Born Free

A woman wrote to a newspaper advice columnist:

"My young family lives in a quiet, respectable neighborhood. Our children are both under five years of age, and we want a safer place for them to play. We moved here because most of the families here are young and we thought other parents would share our interest in good schools and safe streets.

"We are deeply concerned about the rise of juvenile delinquency in this neighborhood. Kids—some of them as young as ten—break into homes here, knife pedestrians, attack old people and the handicapped. And they are not kids from across town—they live right here where they know nothing of hunger or poverty, where they have every opportunity and advantage. Why is this happening? Why is it happening to us in *this* neighborhood? What can we do?"

That plea for help is not a unique one. All across the country parents are worried about their families' safety; many agonize over where they went wrong when their own children turn to crime. School teachers complain of abuses and of the tremendous effort it requires to control their students' behavior. Academics suffer as well. Every year national SAT scores slide a bit, indicating that our high school seniors perform less and less well in basic language and computative skills. Jack Anderson recognized this trend: "Not to take anything away from the decadence of past generations, the America of the 1970s is in a class by itself." Supporting his argument with alarming statistics, he proceeded then to discuss this generation of self-indulgence, listing too-common wrongs that range from faults such as splurging and loafing to crimes such as cheating, stealing, and murdering.

What is happening to us? It appears that we have somehow lost control. Marriage is losing its sanctity, the work ethic seems to have gotten lost, and entertainment standards have sunk to new lows. Even in our own homes decadence is illustrated to our children by means of the television. Have you really *looked* at what your kids watch, or have you yourself perhaps been lulled into acceptance of its violence and poor taste by the very fact that we see so much of it?

We are in the throes of a moral battle without being fully aware of it — of the issues or the cost of it — mostly because it all hinges on the idea of freedom, an idea we fight zealously to protect. Among our freedoms are those principles that allow us to choose our own life-styles and speak our opinions, and that is as it should be. But we must be aware that we choose consequences as well as current activities; and we are responsible for our choices, whatever they may be.

Today we hear from many sources that we should be free from "the harmful myths and hang-ups" which have restrained us in the past. "People are more important than rules or standards," we hear. For many, that translates into "Do whatever feels good; act on your impulses; self-control is old-fashioned, and restricting yourself is harmful." Those who adhere to this philosophy blame "the system" rather than any person or group of persons for such undeniable social ills as poverty and crime. They ignore the weighty matter of responsibility and, in the name of freedom, declare themselves independent of moral law, social standards, educational restrictions, and the notion of right and wrong.

Such a declaration is gross abuse of the concepts of human liberty. No one can make any choice concerning his conduct without accepting the restrictions of its consequence. Freedom means that we *can* choose, but it does *not* relieve us of our responsibility. Said Aleksandr Solzhenitsyn in his 1978 commencement address at Harvard University: "It is time to defend not so much human rights as human obligations. Destructive and irresponsible freedom has (for too long) been granted boundless space."

What has this to do with our lives? A great deal, in terms of self-discipline and decision-making from day to day. Let me give you an example.

I know of one young woman who was seventeen, beautiful, intelligent — and rebellious. Her parents' standards were too strict for her taste, so in her search for freedom she dropped out of high school, left home, and got married. By the age of twenty she was the mother of two and had already faced a scarring divorce. Her former husband wasn't interested in paying child support of any kind, so she was faced with the double challenge of rearing two small children alone and providing for them. Of course, she had no skills to sell in the job market — she hadn't even graduated from high school. As a result, most of the time things were pretty lean. She remembers a time when for three whole weeks the only food she had for herself and her children was a case of chicken noodle soup. For breakfast, lunch, and dinner it was the same — chicken noodle soup. Her children would ask, "Please, Mommy, can't we have something besides soup?" And she could not answer them, because her mind was occupied with the problem of what to do when the soup was gone.

Think of what the other young women her age were doing during that period. For them it was a time of high hopes and dreams for the future, a time of dating and fun. This young woman had chosen freedom instead. In desperation and misery she began to look for escape in the psychedelic world. She turned to drugs and spent every day smoking grass or taking something harder, trying to escape her problems. After all, she was free to do that too.

There were times when she became so spaced out that she wasn't even sure if she existed. She turned to therapy for help; and her therapist confided to her parents that his immediate goal was just to keep her alive. She was that near the brink of suicide.

What a dear price her freedom had cost! At last, when life was so black there seemed to be no hope, she started to pray; but even the Lord seemed unreachable to her. Then one night as she sat at a party, her eyes staring fixedly ahead with the heaviness of a drug upon her, something happened to change her life. All around her in the room was every kind of wantonness; a young man was waiting for her in a dark corner. But suddenly, through all that fog and sin, she seemed to hear a voice. Oh, this voice was not audible, but its message was loud enough.

"Leave this party now, or you will never be able to make that kind of choice again," it seemed to say. She found herself arguing with the message. "Can't I just stay until the end of this one party?"

But the voice came to her strongly again, "Leave this party *now*, or you will never be able to make that choice again." Then, for the first time in five years, she did a wise thing. She got her coat and left the party; and from that day on she started to rebuild her life. Along the way there were setbacks, times when trying to regain her self-control and sense of purpose seemed almost impossible, but she did it. She left all that misery behind.

In view of this girl's experience, is it surprising that scripture refers to ignoring moral law as "the awful chains by which ye are bound"? (2 Nephi 1:13.) *Chains*—what a graphic word! The chains of our habits and weaknesses bind us like slaves when we try to "free" ourselves from responsibility.

Where, then, is *real* freedom—the kind of liberty that gives us a sense of dignity, a feeling of control and influence in our own lives? The answer is in the scriptures: "And ye shall know the truth, and the truth shall make you free." (John 8:32.) It is acknowledgement of the truth—of the eternal laws which govern our behavior—that makes us truly free. The alternative is to be pushed about by whatever whim overtakes us. Can we consider ourselves free if we submit to that?

It may be that mankind in general does not see the Lord's laws as liberating. They may believe that morality is like television's Nielsen ratings—whatever is popular at the moment is what goes, regardless of its merit. But you know better than that. All you have to do is consider the bondage of those who serve every impulse and of those societies that flounder out of control to see the deception in that kind of thinking. So remember and follow what you know is right. Remember what it means to be truly free.

Be Not Afraid

Every one of us has some fear he cherishes, some impending disaster he can't shake loose, some vision of personal pain as a result of world conditions, some magnification of doubts into giant spooks. You know the feeling. Oil prices go up, and your stomach turns over because you're sure you'll be the one who can't get to work all week on one tank. The airplane you're riding in takes a slight bump and you know you're dead—it's just a matter of waiting to hear the crash. A twinge in the chest must be a heart attack; the fact that the kids are fifteen minutes late has to mean an accident or a kidnapping. Maybe it's paying bills that upsets you; perhaps you worry that people don't like you. We all have minor phobias—they are part of what makes us interesting.

In nature, fear is seen as the instinct to survive. Deer run from forest fires; rabbits hide at the first scent of their predators; most creatures avoid contact with man—and well they should. Fear, like pain, is often the unpleasant warning that helps ward off an even less pleasant occurrence.

But fear can grow beyond the useful warning and the amusing characteristic. Fear can become a debilitating habit, carrying with it unnecessary stress and anxiety. The capable student who is frightened in a test can go quite blank and fail. The soldier in the battlefield whose fear freezes him runs a greater chance of being shot. And every one of us who allows his fears of the unknown future, his "what ifs," to crowd today's beauty out of his range of vision, risks leading a joyless life.

When the stock market crashed in 1929, marking the beginning of the Great Depression, many people reacted out of blind panic. Then, as months wore on, a nameless, unreasoning, hopeless fear set in — not the kind of fear that gets people moving to solve the problem, but an enervating, insidious fear that bred inertia and list-lessness. People simply gave up because they were afraid that nothing they tried would help. It was in response to this situation that Franklin D. Roosevelt made the famous comment that we had nothing to fear but fear itself. Certainly the immobilizing fear of that period was a genuine threat. In most cases the fear we suffer over events that might never actually happen is hardly worth de-stroying our present happiness for.

Most fears focus on the future, on conditions that don't yet exist anywhere but in our minds. Some are really quite groundless, and we can discard them if we examine them objectively and rationally, but they can control our lives if we do not. For example, many people fear the number thirteen. Since I am not one of them, I see this particular fear as groundless; it has no control over me. But it can and will control those who cherish it until they themselves scrutinize it for validity.

Sometimes just naming what scares us and facing it squarely is enough to make it go away. If some worry is eroding your happi-ness, maybe it is time to sit down and face some questions: What is the worst thing that could happen to me? What is the real likelihood of its happening? If it does happen, can I possibly survive? In the meantime, what help is it to me to worry about it?

One engineering student at a good university began to fret about his mathematics background. Even though he had qualified to enter the program, he was preoccupied with the idea that he might not know enough math to get through. The more he worried, the harder it was for him to study. He began pushing himself to put in extra hours until he was so exhausted that he got sick and missed several classes. The farther he fell behind, the more he worried. The cycle fed itself until finally he realized his worst fear — he did indeed fail. His fears had become self-fulfilling prophecies.

But here's the amazing part of the story: the lad actually lived after he had flunked out. Not only did he live, he changed his major to political science, went on to law school, and pursued a career he found immensely satisfying. All that brow-wrinkling went for nothing!

I really believe that the fear of failure is the most pervasive in our culture. It may take the form of any of several fears: making mistakes, not pleasing the boss, not making enough money — the list goes on. But it all boils down to fear of failure — a fear that destroys the human spirit, that keeps us from trying, that drains our energies and our self-esteem. And the best way to combat it is to face it, to accept failure at some things we attempt without concluding that we ourselves are total failures.

It is true that those who achieve the greatest success take the greatest risks of failing. They progress by trial and error. They make mistakes, just like all the people who don't achieve very much. But the real successes are those who go on after each mistake. They counterbalance their fears with faith — in themselves, in their goals, in their God — and they bravely proceed even when they are scared. Courage, after all, is not the absence of fear but the ability to confront it and deal with it intelligently, calmly, and determinedly.

The scriptures are full of admonitions to "fear not." The Lord doesn't expect us never to be scared, but he does expect us to develop faith sufficient to overcome our fears and the temptations and troubles that follow them. He quite pointedly discusses the danger of being frightened in Doctrine and Covenants 67:3: "Ye endeavored to believe that ye should receive the blessing which was offered unto you; but behold, verily I say unto you there were fears in your hearts, and verily this is the reason that ye did not receive." Indeed, fear itself is all we need be frightened of, for it can so clog up our minds and hearts that the Lord himself can't get through to bless us. We can get so bound up in our fears that life's sweetest pleasures and challenges remain forever beyond our reach.

How then shall we resist fear? Mainly by faith in measures equal to or greater than our fears. We can also resist it by confronting it, naming it, being rational about its sources and realistic about its effects. Another good idea is to concentrate on making each today work, without cluttering it with the past or the future. The great Canadian physician Sir William Osler suggested this idea to a group of Yale University students by likening each day to the water-tight compartments on an ocean liner. If we divide time into "day-tight compartments" we can touch a button to slam iron doors that will shut out yesterday's trouble. Another button closes out tomorrow's uncertainty, leaving us safe with the manageable day we are living right now. Thus we are safe for today.

May we live in the present and find joy in it.

Time in Your Hands

Are you ever like the man described in this verse?

>He was going to be all a mortal could be . . . tomorrow.
>No one could be kinder or braver than he . . . tomorrow.
>A friend who is weary and troubled he knew
>Would be glad of a lift and needed one too,
>On him he would call and see what he could do . . . tomorrow.
>It was too bad indeed he was busy today
>And had not a minute to stop on his way,
>More time he would have for others, he'd say . . . tomorrow.
>But the fact was he died and faded from view,
>And what he had left when living was through,
>Was a mountain of things he intended to do . . . tomorrow.

Oh, yes—tomorrow! Tomorrow sits there on the horizon looking like a much better day for whatever task or duty is at hand, doesn't it? Tomorrow you'll have time, you'll feel better, you'll have fewer pressures, you'll finish up this project and get around to that one.

But that tomorrow floating on the horizon is just like a mirage. A traveler in the desert trudges along the vast hot sand and sees in the distance a shimmering lake of water. When he trudges to that distant point he finds himself in the middle of vast hot sand, scanning the horizon for another lake of water. Just so, we look to tomorrow; and when we reach it, tomorrow takes on the properties of today. The truth is that we will always look for tomorrow, but we'll never get there—all we have is today.

Consider the fellow who plans each day's activities the night before and resolves to get up at six o'clock in the morning to read the scriptures for a few minutes before getting ready for work. Certainly he's on the right track. But every morning when that alarm rings at six our groggy friend turns it off, yawns, and sinks back into his pillow, thinking: *I'm beat. I have so much to do today that I really need my rest. Tomorrow I'll read.* And he dozes off for an extra thirty minutes. Will he ever get that scripture study accomplished? Of course not, because tomorrow never comes. And today? Today he practiced sleeping till six-thirty. Today he reinforced a habit, he strengthened a behavior pattern. He actually made it *harder* for himself to read those scriptures.

Suppose that today he turned off that six o'clock alarm, yawned, stretched, and forced himself to sit up, rub his eyes, and reach for his scriptures — just *today*. Then he wouldn't have to worry about tomorrow; he would have one more today in which to rub his eyes and reach for the scriptures. But it has to be done *today*.

We all resolve to grow, improve, achieve in one way or another. Who has not decided to diet, to practice the piano, to get organized, to do his genealogical research, to exercise, to maintain a food storage system, to study? It's easy to make such decisions, and to make them enthusiastically. But true character is the result of following through after the enthusiasm has subsided. Those who succeed are those who can act on their resolutions when the mood to resolve has passed. The repeated scriptural admonishments to "endure to the end" refer directly to this ability to act — and to act consistently and continuously — on our resolutions.

The past is gone. It is a chapter already written, a painting completed. We cannot add to it now, nor can we remove from it any word or deed. The future stretches before us, but it is not ours to have. By the time we can touch the future it has become the present — and the present *is* ours. It is all that we have. Today is a new gift from the future which will move irrevocably into the past regardless of what we do or fail to do with it.

Whatever it is that you need to do, do it now. You will never have another chance to make today productive. And once you begin to fill today with the deeds you've promised yourself you'll do, you'll discover that you have eliminated the expenditure of time and effort on procrastination, rationalization, and self-recrimination that waiting for tomorrow entails.

I know of a man who missed his chance. His widowed mother, who lived alone, had yearned for years for an orchid corsage. Now, that doesn't sound like too much to want, does it? She had always loved flowers and delighted in their delicate beauty. He thought it would bring him real joy to take her an orchid—maybe take her out to dinner too. But he was a busy man, an executive in his company. He had children who needed him and important responsibilities. Little things around the house needed fixing. The days just seemed to fill up, and somehow he never got around to getting his mother that orchid. He'd think of it at the wrong times. Today he was always so busy, and he told himself he would get her an orchid tomorrow.

And, you know, he finally did get her that orchid corsage. It rode very beautifully on top of her coffin as it was taken to the cemetery. She never got to pin it on her shoulder or smell its fragrance. He never got to see the light of happiness spark in her eyes when he handed it to her.

Don't miss today waiting for tomorrow. Tomorrow never comes. Take control of your time by making today valuable. It is the only time you have.

Reflections on Womanhood

One of the most significant questions of our day is what it means to be a woman. The news is full of political, social, and legal issues concerning woman. The media make almost daily mention of the injustice of her treatment as a second-class citizen; conferences are convened to discuss her problems; state and federal lawmakers debate her status. It seems to me that, since all this is going on around us, it is important at this time to examine woman's *eternal* standing, to rephrase that question the world is asking. What does it mean to be a daughter of God, a woman-child of our Creator? For an answer to that, let's look at the women in the Savior's mortal life and see what they meant to him.

Of course, the first woman in his life was his mother, and her story begins months before his birth. In Luke we read of the angel's visitation announcing Christ's birth to this young woman of Nazareth, a girl who revered the Father above all things. She was awed by his message: "Hail, thou that art highly favored, the Lord is with thee: blessed art thou among women." (Luke 1:28.)

Those who yearn for the Lord's spirit and search the world for their true identity might look closely at the example of this simple girl. The quality that shines through her personality is her delight in serving her God. It is evident in the poetry of her words of greeting to her cousin Elisabeth:

"And Mary said, My soul doth magnify the Lord,

"And my spirit hath rejoiced in God my Saviour.

". . . for, behold, from henceforth all generations shall call me blessed.

"For he that is mighty hath done to me great things; and holy is his name.

"And his mercy is on them that fear him from generation to generation.

"He hath shewed strength with his arm; he hath scattered the proud in the imagination of their hearts.

"He hath put down the might from their seats, and exalted them of low degree.

"He hath filled the hungry with good things." (Luke 1:46-53.)

That such richness of spiritual understanding could issue from a girl so young gives us some knowledge of Mary. She was well versed in the ancient psalms of her people, yes; but there is something more. She seemed to understand a truth that eludes most of us — that we are ultimately dependent on the Lord for all things. Neither admission to the inner ring of the social elite nor promotion to the board of directors will give us the jubilation we sense in Mary's song of praise. She knew, as few of us know, that it is only the Lord who can fill the hungry and only the Lord who can quench the unidentifiable yearnings that keep us running after worldly goals. Mary, who in her quiet, humble way kept the news of her eternal honor in her heart, exemplifies the finest in all women and men; she recognized, as we must, our need for the Lord to buoy us up through life, acknowledging that no worldly honor can compensate if we have lost sight of him who gave us life.

The spiritual sensitivity so sweetly evident in Mary seems to be a gift of woman's nature. It was Elisabeth, Mary's older cousin, who, through powerful spiritual witness, first recognized Mary's calling without need for words. When Mary learned of her forthcoming motherhood, she hurried to the village where Elisabeth lived, there to spend part of those joyous months. The Bible records that when Elisabeth greeted Mary she said, even before being told of Mary's conditon: "Blessed are thou among women, . . . And whence is this to me, that the mother of my Lord should come to me?" (Luke 1:42-43.)

Elisabeth, who also was with child, showed no jealousy of her younger cousin. Elisabeth entertained in her home for several months the woman who was to bear the Christ, yet she felt no selfish pangs at the realization that Mary's son would be greater than her own. This glimpse of two such angelic mothers scatters to the wind the worldly beliefs that a woman's nature is basically jealous or filled with rivalries. In the miracle of childbirth and motherhood there is a spiritual sisterhood unique to the fair sex, a touch with the eternities that men can rarely understand.

Perhaps it was from his sensitive mother, Elisabeth, that John the Baptist learned the quality of humility that stands as one of the hallmarks of his greatness. We remember his refusal to accept the honors of the crowd, declaring himself only the messenger of Christ, the lachet of whose shoe he was not worthy to unloose. Like many great men, John probably learned his most noble characteristics at the knee of his unselfish mother.

Christ, too, must have learned much from his mother and the other women around him. I think it is significant that the women who were dear to him had such distinct and different personalities from one another. One of the most motivating of Christ's doctrines is that we all have eternal personalities with special spiritual gifts and that there is a stewardship for each unique soul in his kingdom.

Take Mary and Martha, two sisters who lived in the little village of Bethany on the southwest side of the Mount of Olives. How unalike these two were! The house in which the sisters lived was scrubbed to perfection by Martha, an excellent homemaker. She was a hardworking, practical woman who probably mothered her more pensive sister. Mary, I'm sure, did her share of the work, sweeping the dust of the Jerusalem roads from the floors of their home, but she certainly found much more pleasure in serene meditation.

Luke records that one day Jesus, perhaps craving the companionship of spirits in harmony with his, stopped at the home of Mary and Martha on his way to the Feast of Dedication at Jerusalem. Martha, the eager hostess, bustled around her home to make it flawless for the guest they loved so much; but Mary sat at Christ's feet, her spirit swelling as she drank in his spirit. Martha, involved as she was with many duties, asked Christ to bid Mary come and work with her. Jesus responded patiently: "Martha, Martha, thou art careful and troubled about many things: but one thing is needful: and Mary hath chosen that good part, which shall not be taken away from her." (Luke 10:41-42.)

Surely Christ loved Martha and Mary equally, but his loving rebuke to Martha reminds us of an eternal principle that should not blur before our often-poor vision. There is no limit to what the modern Marthas and Marys may become as long as they remember the better part, putting aside worldly goals to bask in the Lord's warmth and to perceive his desires for them. Somewhere between dusting the house and painting a masterpiece, a woman must put first things first and develop her spiritual talents.

With their special gifts of spiritual sensitivity and faith, women were important to Christ at crucial times in his life. It was these same devoted sisters, Mary and Martha, whose brother Lazarus was stricken and died before Christ arrived to save him. Lazarus had lain in the grave four days when Jesus finally arrived in Bethany. Each sister, as she greeted Christ, said with the same simple but saddened faith, "Lord, if thou hadst been here, my brother had not died." (John 11:21, 32.) What belief was expressed in that simple sentence by these great women of faith! What a contrast that faith was to the disbelief and anger of the people of Jerusalem who came to view the drama! Jesus wept before these loving sisters at their bereavement, and perhaps at the lack of faith on the part of the crowd. At this moment, what a comfort was the great faith of the women, Mary and Martha! While they watched, Jesus raised their brother Lazarus from the dead, and he walked forth from his four-day tomb still bound in heavy burial clothes. Seeing firsthand this miracle that told of the greater miracle to come, the sisters understood, as few others of their day, that Christ himself would be resurrected.

And even as Christ's cross was raised against a darkening sky, as the sharp nails tore his tender flesh and the bitter vinegar rolled down his parched throat, he ennobled a woman. He remembered his angelic mother, Mary, and asked his beloved disciple John to protect and love her as his own mother. Was any woman ever less a second-class citizen?

Finally, the greatest event the world has known was witnessed first by a woman. Mary Magdalene, who had been healed by Jesus, came to the sepulchre in the still morning air just before dawn of the third day after the crucifixion. Drawn there to soothe the ache of his death, she came upon Christ's empty tomb. She ran to tell Peter and brought him back to the empty sepulchre. Peter saw the empty tomb and returned home, apparently unaware of what had happened. But Mary remained at the tomb weeping. At last she looked into the sepulchre and beheld two angels in white. "Woman, why weepest thou?" they asked. Mary Magdalene answered, "Because they have taken away my Lord, and I know not where they have laid him." (John 20:13.) Then she turned and saw Jesus, but not until he spoke her name did she realize that Jesus Christ himself stood before her. "Mary," he said, the voice penetrating sweetly to her soul. It was she who spread the joyous word to his disciples that Jesus Christ indeed was risen. (See John 20:16-18.)

What is a woman? Ultimately, it is neither legislatures nor news media that can say who she is. The Lord himself has shown that hers is an eternal soul filled with glimmers and sunsparks of divinity. He has shown us that no one can say she is second-class, for she has unlimited potential. Modern woman, like the Marys and Marthas before her, can have intimate association with Christ himself.

The Lord has promised to the faithful — men and women alike —*all* of his kingdom. And there is no more that can be given than all.

The Reality of Satan

Beliefs, like clothes, go in and out of style. It used to be the thing to believe in ghosts and devils and witches and so forth, but not any more. And there is danger in this trend because the devil *is* real, and it suits him just fine that few believe it. How can he get resistance from people who don't acknowledge his existence, much less his power?

C. S. Lewis explores this psychology in his book *The Screwtape Letters,* a collection of correspondence between an apprentice devil and his expert uncle. In the book, Uncle Screwtape gives advice on tempting and finally capturing a human victim. Part of his advice is to keep the human ignorant of the devil's reality or — if the human begins to suspect that there *is* a devil — to encourage him to picture "something in red tights," the cartoon character with the pitchfork. Nobody can get serious about a cartoon, so it follows that nobody will believe in the devil at all if the cartoon image is all he sees.

It is interesting to me that this same line of reasoning appears in the Book of Mormon, where we read of a devil who will flatter men "and telleth them there is no hell; and he saith unto them: I am no devil, for there is none." (2 Nephi 28:22.) Many people believe this story, but I think it is important to examine its source before taking stock in it.

What do we know about the devil? We know he has many names. He is sometimes called Satan, or Beelzebub, or the Prince of Darkness; but perhaps his most telling name is Lucifer, a son of the morning, for from all we know of him he is one of God's most brilliant children.

We learn from scripture that before we came to earth there was a great council in heaven. Mortality for each man and woman was to be a time of experience, a time of testing. It was to be a time when God's children, without the steady influence of his presence, would raise their own heads and learn to be more like him. It was to be a sort of cosmic going away to school.

Two plans for mortality were presented. Satan, a son of the morning, presented one. His plan was to force all men to be good, to give men no other choice. Surely the astute Satan understood that coerced goodness is not goodness at all, but he wasn't after that anyway. He didn't want to raise up men and women who could stand righteous before God; he wanted only to raise himself up. "All the glory be for me," he suggested in his plan, giving us a clue to his nature.

Jesus Christ championed the other plan, under which all mankind, he said, would come to earth free to choose for themselves righteousness or sin. When this plan was chosen, Satan—history's first sore loser—defected. He chose not to play since he couldn't make the rules; and so he was cast out with those who would follow him, and they were denied mortal bodies and opportunities.

Satan wanted glory and followers. He wants them still. He wants your body and your opportunities. And far from being a comic figure in red tights, he is a psychological genius who is putting all his skill to the task of keeping men and women from the highest freedom—the development of their innate excellence.

Satan has a storehouse of tricks to enslave us, or at least to keep us from realizing those potentials which have been denied him. Let me share with you just three of his tactics, all taken from scripture, so that you will recognize them for what they are, just as you must recognize their originator for what he is.

The first is the "eat, drink, and be merry" tactic. It is very appealing to look at life as a party, to enjoy its pleasures now and ignore its responsibilities. But only the very ignorant believe that party time can go on indefinitely, so Satan has thrown in a little pay-your-dues clause, a suggestion that we can easily justify sin. Satan supports this attitude:

"Eat, drink, and be merry; nevertheless, fear God—he will justify in committing a little sin; yea, lie a little, take the advantage of one because of his words, dig a pit for thy neighbor; there is no harm in this; and do all these things, for tomorrow we die; and if it so be that we are guilty, God will beat us with a few stripes, and at last we shall be saved in the kingdom of God." (2 Nephi 28:8.)

Notice how subtle the tempter is—he admits that God will punish us, but he dismisses that punishment as "a few stripes"; he concedes that the behavior here described is wrong, but he treats it as only a little wrong, as if there were no absolute standard. None of us is perfect, and none of us savors the guilt we feel when we make mistakes. Satan invites us to ignore that guilt and be merry—a prospect which initially may be pleasing to us, but only until we realize the insidious intent with which it is offered.

A second tactic used to tempt us is the "stiff necks and high heads" tactic. This is an appeal to our pride. Here Satan encourages "the wise and the learned and the rich" to believe in their own powers—and which of us would refuse to be counted among those who have wisdom and knowledge? Again Satan takes the truth—that mortals have and should utilize intellect—and perverts it by suggesting that those mortal powers are enough, that we don't need anybody to tell us what to do. This, of course, eliminates divine guidance, whether direct or through prophets, and creates a society of men and women who, in order to appear wise, shun the help God would give.

The third tactic is just as subtle and just as effective. I call it the "sleepy" tactic. "And others will he pacify, and lull them away into carnal security, that they will say: All is well in Zion; yea, Zion prospereth, all is well." (2 Nephi 28:21.) If you are not easily swayed into evil, if you cannot be convinced that you don't need God, if you cannot be made to join Satan, then the least Satan can do is try to keep you from fighting him. And this he does by rocking you securely to sleep, by whispering, "Everything is okay," to you until you nod and yawn and cease to take an active stand against him.

And is there any harm in that? You are not, after all, joining him —so is there a risk in being content? I should say so! The rest of 2

Nephi 28:21 reads this way: "And thus the devil cheateth their souls, and leadeth them away carefully down to hell."

The devil is real, and his genius for trapping you in sin is devious and subtle. Believe it, and resist with all the power you have and all the divine power you may call on.

Communication

Part 4

Word Power

Language is an incredible force in our lives. It makes the difference between communicating with others and isolating ourselves from them. If we don't have command of our language, it can control us and perhaps say more about us than we want revealed.

If you doubt the power of language, listen to these excerpts from accident reports actually submitted to an insurance company and compare what was *intended* with what was actually *said*.

One policyholder reported, "I collided with a stationary truck coming my way."

Said another, "I thought my window was down, but found it was up when I put my hand through it."

I really like this one: "The guy was all over the road; I had to swerve a number of times before I hit him."

Here's an interesting explanation for an accident: "I pulled away from the side of the road, glanced at my mother-in-law, and headed over the embankment."

Finally, one obviously distraught soul included in his accident report this sentence: "I told the police that I was not injured; but on removing my hat, I found that I had a fractured skull."

Aren't words wonderful? They can run away with us foolishly or serve us wisely. They can harm or delight us, clarify or confuse, build or destroy. Their power is unmistakable.

You know this saying; think about its meaning: "I know you believe you understand what you think I said, but I am not sure you realize that what you heard is not what I meant." That sums it up, doesn't it? Words can help us or hinder us in getting through to one another, but we have to rely on them because we have no choice.

For this reason, we need to be careful about the words we choose and the way we use them. Christ himself advised, "Not that which goeth into the mouth defileth a man; but that which cometh out of the mouth, this defileth a man." (Matthew 15:11.)

Too often we become the most eloquent only when we're angry. We hurl words like cannonballs at one another, not realizing that the wounds given by words are just as real, if not just as obvious. And as war brings despair and desolation, vindictive words hurled in accusation can bring devastating results: instead of physical wounds, heartache; instead of rubble, anguish; instead of broken bones, broken hearts. To make matters worse, throwing word-grenades usually destroys *both* parties involved; the one who launches the volley is just as likely to get hit as is his target. Shakespeare warned of it this way: "Heat not a furnace for your foe so hot / That it do singe yourself." (*King Henry VIII.*)

There are some people today who believe that arguing can even be healthy for a marriage. "Get it off your chest," they say. "If you think something, say it, no matter how unbecoming." They really think "clearing the air" is worth the pain it can cause. Beware of such thinking. A word once said lingers almost in the air and always in the heart. It is never quite forgotten.

As the great leader Brigham Young warned: "Some think and say that it makes them feel better . . . to give vent to their madness in abusive and unbecoming language. This, however, is a mistake. . . . When the wrath and bitterness of the human heart are moulded into words and hurled with violence at one another, the fire has no sooner expended itself than it is again rekindled through some trifling course. . . . If this practice is continued, it will lead to alienation between man and wife, parents and children, brethren and sisters, until there is no fellowship to be found." (*Journal of Discourses* 11:255-256.) Words are powerful. What we do or do not say can affect the course of our lives.

We can give joy and satisfaction with words of support, encouragement, approval — but only if we get a chance. First we must be careful not to offend people and send them away with criticism. The unkind thought, once voiced, is difficult if not impossible to eradicate.

So what are you going to do when you feel the urge to say something bitter or stinging to another? Almost everyone feels that way sometimes. We all get hurt; we all become angry. Our defenses just naturally rise when we feel that our self-worth has been stamped into the dust. And when those feelings overtake us, the angry words almost seem to erupt from us. As in Yellowstone's geysers, the pressure builds up and we have to explode. Or do we?

Even in the heat of anger, when the steam is fairly hissing from our throats, we can and must still master ourselves. We do not need to explode or say unkind things. We can simply learn to control the tongue. David recorded his resolve to do so this way: "I will take heed to my ways, that I sin not with my tongue: I will keep my mouth with a bridle." (Psalm 39:1.)

Think of the sad consequences of saying everything that may pass through your mind. Think on that and then control yourself. Just do it. I know a little poem (taken from the Laurel Course A for 1978-1979) that may help you in that task:

> If on occasion you have found
> Your language is in question,
> Improper thoughts flee 'cross your mind,
> Then here's a sound suggestion.
>
> Just hum your favorite hymn,
> Sing out with vigor and vim.
> Resound a note, expound a quote,
> Or hum your favorite hymn.
>
> If words come crashing 'cross your tongue,
> Provoked by angry notions,
> There's one sure way to get control,
> And soothe your seared emotions.
>
> Just hum your favorite hymn,
> Sing out with vigor and vim.

> Resound a note, expound a quote,
> Or hum your favorite hymn.
> (*Learn of Me and Listen to My Words*, p. 51.)

Now, that's good advice. Can you imagine what would happen to families if we all started singing or quoting a verse every time we were about to say something inappropriate? Why, there would be a peaceful tune heard round the world. Wouldn't that be great?

We can do it! I want you to know we can do it! We can learn to control our words and use them to bring joy instead of devastation to others. While this old world struggles under the weight of war, we can bring peace to our homes and to ourselves. We can learn to speak more kindly to mom and dad. We can learn to use words that convey only strength to our friends. We can learn to use our language to bless our children instead of alienate them. It's all in a word.

Don't let the language run away with *you*. Never let your words convey anything but your finest thoughts. It seems such a small thing, but the results of mastering your manner of expression will be far-reaching.

Don't Swear to It

Do you remember Professor Henry Higgins? He is the elegant and skillful linguist in the musical *My Fair Lady*. Just by listening to an Englishman speak, Higgins can pinpoint his birthplace within a mile. Some conversations make him wince, others he listens to with pleasure, as ordinary folk might listen to music. He sums up the matter of language, "An Englishman's way of speaking absolutely classifies him."

How true, Henry Higgins! We judge others and we indeed classify ourselves by that all-important element of first impressions —language. Open your mouth and say "ain't" or "he don't" and you might as well put on a badge that says *illiterate* or *careless*. Want to tell the world your age? Just use an old slang term—call a guy a "square," tell someone to "scram," describe a movie as "the cat's meow," or tell your friend his tie looks "groovy"—nothing will date you faster. Even calling something "cool" isn't cool any more. When I was a teenager the term was "zorchy"—figure that out!

Children use name-calling to hurt one another. "Dummy!" they shout at the person they're angry at. And it's easy to see that this kind of language use is more a release of emotion for the shouter than a real punishment of the other party. The child just as often shouts, "Dummy!" at the toy he trips over or the door that bumps him, and what does the door care? Come to think of it, adults do the same thing. Don't you say, "Dummy!" to the guy who cuts in front of you in traffic, even though you know he can't hear you?

Language is also a tool for classing up our acts. Many people search for the most complicated way possible to express an idea, apparently assuming that (at least in terms of syllables) more is most impressive. It is said that Churchill once accused his opponents in Parliament of "terminological inexactitude." Now, *there's* a fancy way to call a man a liar!

Euphemisms creep into all phases of our lives. Yesterday's dear old cow barn is today's "milking parlor"; the poor and the ignorant are now "underprivileged"; and instead of dying, people "pass away," "pass on," or "succumb." If the dog catcher would rather be an "animal welfare officer," and the trash collector prefers to be a "garbologist," who's to complain? It's all a matter of language.

No doubt about it — whether it's slang or poetry, simple or elaborate, your language classifies you faster than anything else. That's why I'm so surprised at the number of otherwise refined and gentle people who degrade themselves by swearing, telling coarse stories, and — worst of all — taking the Lord's name in vain. They must know that in doing so they stamp themselves as vulgar! The so-called "four-letter words" are used by the cheapest and most pitiable in society. Why would the mature, the sophisticated, the educated, want to use them too? Any schoolteacher can tell you that it is the childish student who scrawls filth on the walls, not the one who regards others' feelings. The gracious and the well bred don't need such expressions.

A friend of mine was at a special baseball function some years ago and observed an interesting scene. There on the stand were a fine religious leader and one of baseball's greats. The audience was packed with players and coaches from all over the country just waiting to hear from the famous athlete. Under the influence of the men in that audience would be many thousands of American youth, youngsters just hanging on their every word and gesture. That's quite a responsibility!

It came time for the player to present his workshop. He rose to the stand, pulled down a screen and began talking about how to teach boys to hit, referring to slides projected on the screen that showed batting stance and eyeing the ball. The crowd was intent on the athlete's every word. He knew his stuff. He'd proved it over and over again against stiff competition in baseball games. But the projectionist had decided to play a trick on the athlete by inserting slides of undressed women among the baseball pictures. At first the athlete was taken aback as the crowd laughed, but then he joined in with the guffaws and crude remarks. The language of both the athlete and the audience grew more profane, and what had started out as a fine, high-minded presentation was degraded by uncouth language and implications.

The religious leader on the stand was clearly unhappy about the tone of things. He shifted uncomfortably in his seat and stared at his feet. He felt as if his presence there was an endorsement of what was going on, but he could hardly leave — his name was on the program.

Now, what would you do, if you'd been there? Join in and be a part of the group? After all, nobody likes to be an outcast. Would you maybe slip away silently, so as not to be noticed?

As the athlete finished his talk, he was met with thundering applause and a standing ovation. Other professional players themselves were coming up to get his autograph.

When the noise had died down and the crowd had returned to their seats, it was finally the religious leader's turn to say a word. This is what he said: "You were terrific tonight; I learned some things about the game that I'd never known before. Thanks for a great experience. Now I want to tell you something else, too. When I was a youngster, you were one of my idols. I used to collect baseball cards, and I'd trade other players away so I could have every picture of you in my collection. I'd stand in front of the mirror by the hour and try to copy your stance, your every move. Could I really be your friend?

"But tonight you fell off your pedestal. I never expected to hear you say such things. Every time you opened your mouth, you offended a lot of people. You're so great; you don't have to do that."

The athlete stammered for a minute and then said, "I—uh—thank you. Nobody's ever talked to me like that before." He considered it a favor. He, who had spent his whole life reaching for great things, didn't want his language to classify him as anything less. Do you? Do you want to struggle for excellence only to be hanged by your own tongue as it utters profanity?

When one of the dearest men I know had just been operated on in the hospital and was being wheeled back to his room in a hospital bed, he taught this same principle. He was still heavily sedated, but he was conscious enough to hear the words of the young intern who had caught his hand between the elevator door and the mobile bed. The intern took the Lord's name in vain, and my dear friend, as weak as he was, raised his head and said in kindly rebuke, "Oh, please don't talk that way about my best friend."

Well, the intern must have grown up a little right there, for he said: "I'm sorry, sir. I won't do that any more."

If profanity should ever come into your mind, let it wither away without utterance, for your own sake. Never—for any reason— take the Lord's name in vain. It cheapens you, it insults him, and it offends those of us to whom he is a best friend. Make him your friend, and always speak as you would to him.

The Best-seller to Discover

There was once an old professor of English who retired from her position at a small New England college and moved into a tiny fishing village on the coast. She had not been there long before it became evident to her that many of the adults in the village were quite illiterate. The children all attended school, but many of their parents and grandparents could neither read nor write. Energetically she promoted reading lessons for them at the school and, even though she did not teach them herself, she was very interested in the progress they made with the school teacher.

One warm morning as she was walking along the main street she met one of the new "students." Said she, "Well, Mr. Locke, I suppose you can read your Bible pretty well by now."

"Bless you, ma'am," replied the man gratefully, "I got past the Bible and into *Sports Illustrated* way last week."

How many of us think we have better things to read than the Bible? I'm afraid there are too many. We learn Bible stories as children, we memorize a few passages, and we keep a Bible on the bookshelf at home and call it good. But that is not enough. If we rely on retold versions of the stories and never read the words ourselves, how can the words bear witness to us of their truth?

We live in a society of scriptural illiterates, a society of people who know Charlton Heston but not Moses. We read less than earlier generations did because we have other media to inform and entertain us; and when we do read, what do we choose? The funnies. Best-selling novels. Jogging guides. Recipes. Maintenance handbooks. Certainly there is no harm in such materials, but they are not so terrific that they should supersede God's eternal truths.

Look at the way people clamor after all those self-help books published every year. They can hardly wait to find out how to assert themselves, succeed in business, have a better marriage, save at the grocery store, tone up their stomach muscles, cut their taxes, learn faster, understand themselves, cope better. What if all that good stuff were in one place? What if the clues for being successful and healthy and really happy were in a single volume? And what if that volume carried the bonus of promised spiritual help to understand it? Well, you know what I'm getting at: those "what ifs" are realities, and the book is the Bible.

Do you know enough about this book? Do you realize that most of the famous Old Testament stories are contained in Genesis? Have you no curiosity about the rest of it? How well do you know Habbukuk? When was the last time you read Paul's epistles? Shouldn't you understand Revelation? Imagine yourself as the soul in Carol Lynn Pearson's poem "The Lord Speaks to a Literary Debauché Newly Arrived in Heaven."

> Impressive indeed, this shelf of books
> On which all the earth-critics dote.
> But oh, my son, how I wish that you
> Had read the book I wrote.
> (From *Beginnings*, Doubleday, 1967, p. 13.)

The scriptures are ours primarily as a way for us to know God and receive his guidance. Scripture study is one of the conditions upon which we are promised eternal life. We are admonished to "press forward, feasting upon the word of Christ" (Nephi 31:20), but most of us barely nibble at this tremendous resource for comfort and direction.

If we agree that we *should* read the Bible, why don't we do it? Perhaps because eternal life seems to be a long way away — especially compared to the work for which we need to read other things by next Wednesday. Maybe we put off reading the Bible because we doubt the immediate benefits of that study or because we suspect that it might be pretty boring. But how can we knock it until we've tried it? Let me strongly recommend to you T. Edgar

Lyon's article "The New Testament — Why Read It?" in the February 1973 issue of the *New Era.* Two of the examples of Bible readers he cites are the great orators Senator William Borah and President Calvin Coolidge.

What advantage has Bible study for a senator? Said Borah: "I read the Bible, particularly the New Testament, to learn how to say what I feel must be said clearly, distinctly, and with effectiveness. The Bible writers didn't waste words. . . . They convey great ideas, but stated simply enough to leave no doubt what they intended to say. The Bible has helped me, more than anything else I've read or studied, to speak effectively, using a minimum number of words to convey my ideas with vigorous, descriptive words."

President Coolidge found similar merit in reading the Bible when he was a boy. He had entered an essay contest asking for a history of the United States during its first century and a half. The essay was to stress those factors that had influenced the development of the nation during that period and — here was the catch — it was to be no longer than five hundred words.

Many entered the contest, but most dropped out, declaring the assignment impossible. But young Coolidge wrote a prize-winning essay without any difficulty; and he explained his win by surmising that his competitors had not studied the Bible, a book he considered to be an excellent model for concise statement. He went on to issue a challenge of his own to illustrate his point: could anyone write a briefer account of the parable of the Good Samaritan without leaving out any detail of the story?

The Bible is not a drag. It is not cod-liver oil reading, the kind that has to be suffered through because it is good for you. On the contrary, the Bible is magnificent literature — it contains beautiful poetry and songs, terrific action stories, political intrigue, touching love stories, and great wisdom. Not only does it teach religion, it is a primary record of the culture, history, philosophy, and ethics of the Western world.

And it *is* unmistakably the way to eternal life. Said Jesus, "Search the scriptures; for in them ye think ye have eternal life: and they are they which testify of me." (John 5:39.) If eternal life seems a long way off, consider that *today* is part of eternity and that — as I suggested before — all the clues to a fulfilling life, now and forever, are contained in the scriptures.

Sometimes mortality frustrates us. We feel blunted, somewhat powerless, cut off from the Lord. We utter prayers, often wondering if they have done more than merely echo in our heads. We want desperately to understand who the Lord is, what he can do for us, and what he expects of us. We'd like to slice through all these layers of blindness and dailiness which seem to keep us bound. There is something deep in our very nature which seems to whisper that there is more.

It is only through scripture study and prayer that we can gain a higher concept of the character and will of our Heavenly Father. In the pages of scripture we see intimately how he grooms his children for their best growth. As we read his words and admonitions again and again, the light of our understanding opens. Principles we thought we understood suddenly take on new dimension.

"They are they which testify of me," he said of the scriptures. Isn't that really what our hungry souls are yearning for: to know Christ, to begin to have his divine nature revealed to us, to begin to perceive clearly those characteristics which we now perceive only in part?

It took the apostles of Jesus Christ during his earthly ministry long exposure to him to even begin to comprehend him. Peter had seen Christ take the lifeless hand of a child and raise her from the dead; he had supped with Christ and walked with him; he had dared to step upon the treacherous waves of Galilee to follow him in faith. After all those personal experiences Christ could ask him, "But whom say ye that I am?" (Matthew 16:15.)

Do you know your Savior? Will you recognize him when you do see him if you don't learn to know him now? There is no better way to get acquainted with him than by studying the scriptures. There is no other way to receive his comfort and wisdom to help you cope with your trials than by prayerful attention to the holy record of his dealings with men. Receive his word. Read your Bible.

Prayer That Connects

Have you ever listened to a child's prayer? If ever there was a simple, direct, and beautiful communication, it is the prayer of a child. Often the matter-of-fact expressions of the trials of the very young make us smile, like that of the little Jewish boy who asked God if he had found learning Hebrew so very hard too. I once read a letter from a little girl to God which said: "Are boys better than girls? I know you are one, but try to be fair."

A child's approach is refreshing. Kids say it the way they see it. They talk to God as they would to a "real person"—one who might hear them, understand them, and respond to them. Do you notice a little nugget of truth there?

I often wonder what it is that is missing in the prayers of adults who say such things as, "I just can't get through, my prayers don't connect"; or, "My prayers never get beyond the ceiling." I think I've concluded that these feelings result from a failure to share thoughts, to bare one's soul, to ask exactly the questions that prey on the mind.

Do you recall the place in Mark Twain's *Adventures of Huckleberry Finn* where Huck discovers that you can't pray a lie? He gives it up altogether because what is *really* in his heart doesn't seem appropriate, and he just can't pray anything but the unvarnished truth. How many of us are willing to pray what seems proper rather than what is honest? Do you offer a duty prayer—a few hurried words at the end of a wearisome day? Do you ever get so locked up in the "thank thee's" and "bless me's" that you never get around to anything that really matters to you? In the midst of a struggle to overcome weakness do you share your frustrations or do you summarize, "Help me to do better."

One young man was very much impressed with the account of an ancient prophet who went into the wilderness and prayed all day long and into the night, crying unto the Lord that he might be heard. Well, our young friend thought he'd try the same thing, so he went up into the mountains for an afternoon of prayer. After fifteen minutes he was beginning to search for something to say, and after twenty-five minutes he was flat out of words. Yet this same young man had just the week before spent a whole night long talking to a college roommate about a problem he had. What's the difference? I think it has something to do with really believing we're talking to somebody, rather than filling out thank-you notes and grocery lists of items needed from a cosmic butler.

God is, after all, our father. Imagine how your dad would react if all you ever said to him was: "Hi. I sure appreciate the good name you gave me and all those meals and new shoes over the years. I really need a ten-dollar bill and a word of encouragement. Thanks a bunch. Bye." If your mortal father yearns to counsel with you, to hear the details of your life, to share the happy moments and the griefs, to comfort you, to listen to you, to advise you, how much more must your Eternal Father want to do so!

We are talking here about communicating with a very real (however divine) parent, one who loves us and knows us by name. We don't need to impress him with our eloquence or cleverness in prayer. We don't need to become frozen before him, our hearts stiff with formality. We just need to talk to him and tell him that we love him. We just need to report to him about our day, to tell him about our disappointments and ask for help to be braver and better. Why should it be so hard? Is there something we forget in growing up that children grasp instinctively?

A little blonde-haired four-year-old said in prayer one night, "Bless me not to be scared when the wind blows tonight." It seems she lived in a windy little town, and when the breezes started to whip up at night they rattled against the siding on her house and whistled up the chimney. Her little prayer was so honest, so specific. Do you think the Lord would ignore such a plea?

I'm sure that each of you has a minor if not a major crisis in your life right now. You are worried about the future. It is more and more difficult each month to pay the bills. Maybe your marriage has rough spots or your children seem disobedient. What do you do? You talk to the Lord about it, as if he were there (which, indeed, he is). This doesn't mean listing your petitions and then calling it good. It means that you talk; you pour out your feelings. Nothing is too trivial for the Lord to hear: if something is important to you, I promise you that it is important to him too.

An ancient prophet counseled:

"Cry unto him when ye are in your fields, yea, over all your flocks.

"Cry unto him in your houses, yea, over all your household, both morning, mid-day, and evening.

"Yea, cry unto him against the power of your enemies.

"Cry unto him over the crops of your fields, that ye may prosper in them.

"Cry over the flocks of your fields, that they may increase.

"But this is not all; ye must pour out your souls in your closets, and your secret places, and in your wilderness." (Alma 34:20-22, 24-26.)

The point is that we should involve the Lord in our lives, in every homely detail of our daily progress. Our communication with the Lord is only as meaningful as we make it. If we talk to him about our lives in vague, general terms, repeated again and again, we can pass through mortality without ever experiencing the closeness real prayer can bring.

I have appreciated the responsibility of Church assignments in my life because that responsibility causes me to be totally dependent on my Heavenly Father. Many times a day I draw the curtains in my office and fix the latch on the door so I can kneel down and talk to my Heavenly Father.

The Lord loves you and yearns for you to talk to him. You can stop in the middle of the busiest day to ask for his blessings or to thank him for a lovely morning. He doesn't really care how poetically you put it. He just wants to know it's from you.

I urge you to do so, facing life with your hand in his.

You Never Listen

Thomas Edison worked long and hard to perfect the incandescent lamp; and when he had it, he quite naturally wanted the world to know about it. His idea for letting the public in on his invention was to light up a square mile of New York City; his problem was getting the city's permission. Finally he invited a group of city officials to his plant, where he quietly ushered them into a room dimly lit by a single lamp. He paused a few moments in the semidarkness, then said in a dramatically hushed tone, "Throw the switch." Brilliant light from a string of lamps flooded the room, revealing a glittering table set for a banquet. His guests gasped and, much impressed, granted permission: a square mile of New York City would indeed be lit by Edison's lamps.

It's interesting to me that Edison's tactics were not to explain his idea but to get the attention of a few people who mattered. We all go to great lengths to get the attention of a few who matter, don't we? Children throw tantrums, teenagers rebel, some of us shout or slam doors or send flowers—all because we do not want to be ignored. Just as advertisers put up billboards and politicians pass out handbills, every one of us has a way of saying in his personal life, "Now that I have your attention. . . ." We feel strongly the need to be heard; we crave the ear of the important people in our lives. It is common in the relationships between husbands and wives, employees and bosses, and parents and children to hear again and again these complaints: "You never listen to me." "Didn't you hear what I said?" "You don't understand."

Strange, isn't it, how *everybody* complains that *nobody* listens? Andre Gide is supposed to have opened a lecture once by saying, "All this has been said before — but since nobody listened, it must be said again." Nobody listens. That includes me, and it includes you. Each of us believes himself to be the exception to that rule and, at times, a victim of it; but each rarely makes an honest assessment of his own listening skills.

Maybe one reason we don't consider the possibility that we might be poor listeners ourselves is that we don't want the responsibility that implies. We all know how awful it feels to be ignored. Which of us would be willing to admit that he inflicts such pain on those around him? I read once of a manufacturing plant that developed a serious quality control problem. Months passed, and a large sum of money was spent before the solution came from a young tradesman. This young man finally went to the personnel manager and told him he'd known from the beginning how to correct the problem, but no one would listen to him. He was so frustrated that he was just about to resign his job. "I tried to talk to the foreman and the plant engineer, but they wouldn't listen to me. I finally gave it up because they made me feel like such a dummy." I'll bet neither the foreman nor the engineer would be proud of that, and I'm sure neither would want to take the blame for the cost of all those weeks' work.

Maybe another reason we don't believe ourselves to be poor listeners is that we don't recognize listening as the kind of skill we need to spend time and energy practicing — we may think there's nothing to it. The fact is that listening — not just hearing, but really *listening* — is a lot more demanding than it looks. Did you know that researchers indicate that listening requires extra physical energy? It does — listening makes your heart beat faster, so your temperature goes up and your circulation increases.

Good listening also requires mental energy — not to keep up, but to slow down, to concentrate on what's being said. You see, our minds race along at an incredible pace — much faster than anyone can speak. The average person can say something like 125 words a minute, but he thinks at about four times that rate. This means that in any conversation the listener's mind may be only 25 percent engaged in what is said—he can be thinking his own thoughts and drawing his own conclusions, letting his mind dart back and forth and formulating what *he* will say when it is his turn. He must really work at giving his full attention to *listening*—otherwise, in all that mental zipping around, he's likely to miss the point, draw a wrong conclusion, or alienate the speaker.

And it is that speaker—that fellow who needs to talk to us—who is really at the center of all this. Just as we all want to be heard, we all want to be the kind of friend or mate or parent that someone can confide in. We'd like to be the person who really understands, the one who truly seems to care and know, when the rest of the world is rough and careless. The secret to becoming that person is learning to focus on the *other* guy.

In his novel *Daniel Martin,* John Fowles describes a character who divides his conversation into two categories: "when you speak, and when you listen to yourself speak." Don't you know someone like that? Can't you tell when the person you're talking to turns the volume way down so he doesn't hear you any more but follows his own thoughts? Don't you hate it? Then don't you do it!

You know the cartoon in which the husband goes about his business or reads the newspaper and all the time answers his wife's every comment with the same, "Hmm, hmm; that's nice, dear"—even when she announces that she's moving to Afghanistan. I know a woman who wanted so desperately to have her husband hear her message that she resorted to writing him long letters and leaving them on his pillow at night. "I just couldn't get his attention any other way," she explained. "Every time I tried to talk to him about my needs or my frustrations he would be so ready with his own arguments and defenses that he could not hear what I said."

Who's trying to get through to you? Who is it that considers you one of a few who matter and needs you to hear him? What impediments of your own prevent you from giving that attention? Try an experiment. Just for today, drop your obsession with your own needs and distractions long enough to listen to those around you. Listen to them not just with your ears or your mind, but with your heart. What are they trying to say, however faulty the wording? What are their needs? Why are they bothering to tell you what they tell you? Is there some unspoken message there?

And when you have mastered the art of listening to the mortals you meet, try listening to the Lord. When we pray we are full of advice and requests. We tell him just how to run the universe, and we expect him to jump at our needs like a cosmic bellboy. When was the last time you prayed with few words and an open heart to hear him? When did you talk to him and then remain kneeling, just listening for his response? Too many of us refuse to listen until he performs some wonder in our lives, some miracle of the fish and the loaves. We expect him to do a trick for us and then say, "Now that I have your attention. . . ."

Your attention is no sacrifice to give to those who need to be heard or to those whom you need to hear. With just a little effort you can learn volumes and build trust in important relationships. If only you will listen.

On Taking Offense

One morning I saw a young mother leave her home and start up the block with her little daughter. The child had obviously been crying — her face was still tear-streaked, and she sniffled a bit as she toddled along with her mom. An older woman met them on the sidewalk and said to the mother, "My, but your little girl has a long face."

"She does not!" came the reply sharply. "She's just a bit sad right at the moment."

Now, I'm sure the older woman meant just that: the child did look sad. She was only trying to make conversation; the comment was harmless enough. But the mother believed she was saying that the little girl's face was physically long — as if she resembled a horse, perhaps — and she was much offended.

After watching that little scene, I began to wonder how often we take offense where none is intended and perhaps offend someone else in turn. It appeared to me that this mother had brought some hard feelings with her when she stepped outside of her door that day, and before long she had passed them on to one who didn't deserve them.

It is easy to misunderstand a comment, to misread a look. We magnify a neighbor's harmless remark into a deep-seated dislike. We begin to feel left out, rebuffed, snubbed, put down — only because of our own misinterpretation of some word or gesture. And then our bad feelings can spill over into *our* words and gestures, spreading themselves among our friends and families.

Sometimes we don't like ourselves very well, so we assume that nobody else likes us either. We know our faults and weaknesses, and we feel as if every inadequacy flashes like a neon sign across the forehead; everybody must see it. But the truth is that everybody *doesn't* see our flaws — if someone stumbles upon one of your vulnerabilities, it's probably an accident. Most people don't lie awake at night plotting and scheming to make someone else look bad.

I'm reminded of the greeting a guest gave the bridegroom's parents at a wedding reception. "I didn't receive an invitation to the wedding," she said, "but I decided to come anyway. I knew you meant to invite me, but the invitation was probably lost in the mail or you simply overlooked me in your busyness."

The bridegroom's parents gave her a hug and the assurance that she was right. They loved her and had meant to invite her, but the truth was that they had totally forgotten her in drawing up the list. It was an oversight, a simple human error — nothing more. So, instead of feeling neglected or rebuffed, instead of holding a grudge against the family which could have lasted for years, this guest decided not to take offense.

I'm not necessarily recommending such a procedure for every social event to which you're not invited — hostesses can't very often cope with uninvited guests. But I do want you to note the spirit here. The woman knew better than to feel left out. It was a luxury she simply couldn't afford.

We all indulge in this luxury from time to time — we assume that, because we are conscious of ourselves, everyone is conscious of us. And that's really a pretty self-centered attitude, isn't it? Suppose you don't get the warm greeting you expect from a friend. Is it because he means to be cold to you? Has he singled you out for abuse? Or is he perhaps having a rotten day? Could it be that he is preoccupied with his own problems, completely unrelated to you? Just before you cross this fellow off your list, stop to consider whether you're thinking of yourself or of him. At such moments your gesture of understanding could strengthen that friendship, while your decision to take offense could destroy it.

There is a fable about Jupiter's capricious gift to mankind of special eyeglasses. Each person received his own spectacles, and each pair was different. One was green, another lavender, the next blue, another pink; every pair revealed the world to its owner in a manner quite different from the view of any other person. Nevertheless, every person was delighted with his own glasses and believed them to be the best; and all were satisfied that they saw a true image of life, even though no two were the same.

Each of us looks at the world through his own colored glasses and, because they tint things a different color, we must be wary of the judgments we are likely to make regarding others. After all, the only people whom we mortals never mistake are dead. None of us can pronounce authoritatively on the meaning behind another's actions. No one of us can say that his virtue is the only virtue, that his opinion is the only one.

Scientists have discovered a substance they call the tolerance chemical. Its technical name is phenyl-thio-carbimide. One out of five persons tasting it finds it tasteless, 65 percent find it bitter, 5 percent call it sour, 2 percent insist that is is sweet, and 5 percent are sure it is salty. Others call it something else. There is no one flavor upon which all can agree, because to different people the chemical truly tastes different.

Life is a little like that tolerance chemical. What may be bitter to one may be sweet to another. It is safest and healthiest to assume that even when we are tempted to feel offended no offense was intended. It is most Christian to assume that no one is out to get us, that no one purposely intends to cause us grief.

Now, let's consider for a moment an exception to that general assumption. Let's pretend that someone *does* want to hurt us, to exclude us, to insult us. It usually isn't a very hard task, is it? Most of us are a little vulnerable *somewhere*, and a person making a real effort to offend could probably succeed eventually with any of us. What if that happened? Would it mean that we, the offended party, were in the wrong? Only if we allow ourselves to respond in the wrong.

We have no control over another person's intentions—for good or for evil—but we can control our responses. We can resolve to believe the best about the people we meet, regardless of their true intent. We can choose to understand rather than judge, to accept rather than condemn, to listen with our hearts before we answer. It takes maturity and practice to respond always with love, but we *can* learn it with patience.

Three women were once asked how they handled it when they had been offended in some way. The first admitted that it was difficult for her to forgive someone who made her feel small. She said she carried the sting with her for months until time did its part to ease her feelings.

The second woman said that when she was offended she went to the person boldly and forthrightly with her complaint. Confrontation was the only way for her. Then, she explained, after the issue had been talked out, it was easier for her to forgive.

The third woman gave the most interesting answer of all. What did she do when she was offended? "I just don't take offense," was her reply. "No one can make you feel offended unless you're willing to let them."

The Cheering Section

Have you ever noticed the difference a cheering section makes? Some time ago I saw an NCAA basketball regional match between two teams—one clearly considered the underdog, the other a heavy favorite. The two teams had met each other earlier in season play, and the underdog had been soundly whipped. Everyone expected this game to be the same.

Fan support was about evenly divided between the two teams until halftime, but while the teams were off the floor an incident there seemed to turn the crowd against the team that had been highly favored to win. When the underdog team came onto the floor to begin the second half, the crowd was with them—over fifteen thousand fans jumped to their feet. After that, every basket for that team brought a deafening roar. The noise was almost unbearable. Well, as you might have guessed, the underdog won that game by two points and went into the finals.

A cheering section makes a big difference. As you watch the World Series, or the pro-football playoffs, or the NBA finals, you can be assured that in almost every case the home team will do well. Brazil has a soccer team that rarely loses when it is playing at home. The reason? Marcana Stadium in Brazil holds over 220,000 fans who scream their support at every game. And sports franchises are bought and sold according to the degree of home-town support.

Wouldn't it be fine to feel that kind of support—that twenty-thousand-screaming-fans kind of approval—for your daily work? You have those days when you feel like the underdog. Couldn't you pull through like a champ even on those days if you had a crowd cheering you on?

Well, I believe that you do. You do have a cheering section, both seen and unseen, and their roar can help you succeed if you'll tune your ears to it. It includes those people you see every day who love you—parents, children, friends, teachers, neighbors, co-workers, relatives. And it includes many whom you don't see—heavenly parents, loved ones who have passed on, those who are yet to come. They all want you to succeed. They are pulling for you every day.

I'm sure you know this football story, but I believe it bears retelling. There was a young man who wanted very much to play football. Each of the four years he was in college he tried out for the team. He tried hard, but he just wasn't fast enough—he just didn't have the moves. So for four years he was on the meat squad —he scrimmaged during the week, and he sat on the sidelines during the games.

During this boy's senior year his team was on its way to a conference title. The week before the last big game a telegram arrived for this young man, with the sad news that his father, who had been sick a long time and blind for many years, had finally died. The telegram came while he was at practice, so it was his coach who handed it to him. Soberly the boy read it, showed it to his coach, and said, "I'll have to go home for a couple of days, coach, but I'll be back Saturday for the game."

"It's all right, son," the coach answered, "you just go. Don't worry about football this week."

But the boy was back Saturday morning, pleading and insisting that he be allowed to play. The coach listened to him and reasoned with himself: *The kid's been through a lot at home this week, and he's worked out here for four years without complaining. What harm can he do us on the kick-off?* And he sent the boy in.

The opposing quarterback took the kick-off on the goal line and started up the field, but he was nailed on the seventh yard line. The boy who couldn't make first-string had dropped him in his tracks. The coach left him in the game and watched dumbfounded as the young man set a record in downfield blocking. He was much responsible for the team's championship win that afternoon.

Afterwards, when the locker-room celebration was over, the coach found this young fellow alone. "Son," he said to him, "I don't get it. You played today like an all-American—in four years I've never seen you do anything like it. What happened?"

"Well, coach," the boy replied, "you remember that telegram I got last week."

"Yes."

"It meant that today was the first time my dad could see me play football. I played for him."

This young man knew where his cheering section was; he heard the shouts of support and praise clear from beyond the veil. Every one of us has such support. Even when you feel all alone, there are those who are rooting for *you*.

I remember a friend of mine who went to high school and college, then got married and had a small family. One day a little-known acquaintance of his came up to him and said: "I know you don't know me very well, but I am one of your greatest fans. I have always watched you and have tried to pattern my life after yours. I just thought you might like to know." There are people who care even when we don't know it. I wonder how many parents pray silently for their kids? How many sons and daughters must silently pull for their mom or dad? In how many crises do friends silently cheer for each other? I am convinced that they are many.

Of course, there's only one thing better than to root silently: it's to root both silently and vocally, to let those around us know we really care for them and believe in them. The great American author Nathaniel Hawthorne had such a cheering section. On the day in 1849 when he lost his government job at the custom house, he went home very discouraged. But his wife was rooting for him. When she had heard his story and sympathized with him, she brought him pen and ink and paper and said, "Now you will have time to write your novel." She believed in him, and the result was a classic: *The Scarlet Letter.*

I'm sure there are those who really don't get much support, silent or otherwise. To you in particular I want to give my assurance that there are those who cheer from on high. God created us and loves us. More than anything else, he desires our righteous success now and our safe return to him later. When we feel no other support, we can count on him. David of old told us: "Wait on the Lord: be of good courage, and he shall strengthen thine heart." (Psalm 27:14.)

To all of us who are trying to do the right things, the Lord has again promised, "I will go before your face. I will be on your right hand and on your left, and my Spirit shall be in your hearts, and mine angels round about you, to bear you up." (D&C 84:88.)

And finally, if we can just remember those great promises, we will eventually be able to say, as did Moses, "The Lord is my strength and song, and he is become my salvation: he is my God." (Exodus 15:2.) When all else fails, God will not.

All of us have parents, friends, or other loved ones, who have passed away. They too exercise faith in our behalf. Do parents stop caring because they die? Are friends no longer friends at death? Does caring stop at the grave? I want you to know that it does not. Life is eternal.

And what of those yet unborn? Do they have an interest in your success? Your unborn children watch you from above with great interest and concern. They want the best for themselves and for you. You can be sure of it. Millions of spirits yet to be born cheer loudly for the millions of us who prepare the way for them. It could be no other way.

I hope my message to you is clear. Every person has a cheering section composed of those around him, those who have passed over to the other side, and those who are yet to come. No one is without such support.

Above all, I bear my testimony that there is a Father in Heaven who put you here and wants you back. His support alone will do it. May we draw close to him so we can know it. May we then give it to those around us who need it, especially our own families. May the Spirit give you the same assurance that I have: that our Father lives, that he loves us, and that he, together with many others, can bring us safely home.

The Magic Art of Changing Your Mate

Have you heard the marriage counselor's advice about waterbeds? He says they are bad for your relationship—too many couples are drifting apart!

The divorce rate in our country is no laughing matter, though. It hovers right around 38 percent—much too high. And it indicates not only broken homes, but also broken hearts—for which of us does not marry with a heart full of hope and love and enthusiasm? We've all heard the common bitter complaint, "I gave him (or her) the best years of my life!" And the truth is that that's just what each of us sets out to do—to give the best years of our lives to the mates who will make those years our best.

Sometimes the romantic mist doesn't rise far enough for a couple to see the realities of daily survival until they are long past the honeymoon. They may find themselves gazing wearily across the dinner table at each other, while the children wail and the bills stack up, wondering, *Did I do this to you, or did you do this to me?* One idealistic bride set this as one of her goals: At least once a day, I'll tell my husband I love him. After ten years of marriage and lots of experience with chicken pox and mumps, house payments and dead water heaters, PTA and Boy Scouts, she modified that goal: At least once a day I'll speak to my husband—if only to say that his check bounced.

"To be happy at home is the ultimate result of all ambition," said Samuel Johnson. Perhaps it is because happiness at home is so very important to us that it is sometimes so hard to achieve. We want harmony and peace; we want everything to be perfect; we dream up the ideal for our most important environment. And then, when the real situation doesn't quite measure up, we are doubly disappointed.

This pattern of expecting too much and then being too disappointed is the source of what I believe causes most break ups: Disloyalty, plain, old-fashioned disloyalty. I don't mean the kind of disloyalty that expresses itself in lies or in sleeping around. I'm talking about a much more subtle and insidious disloyalty — disloyalty of the heart and spirit.

There is in many of our hearts a silent criticism of the one we married. You see, we had it in mind that we were going to marry someone perfect, and not for a single one of us did it turn out that way. We ended up marrying someone human, someone with strengths and weaknesses and with some patterns of behavior that may be totally different from ours. When we discover that, when we see those variations from our ideal glaring at us, there is a part of us that is very disapproving and downright disappointed. So we decide to fix things. We are sure that our marriage will be a thousand times sweeter when we have changed our mate, when we have remade our partner in our own image.

I heard of one young couple who got married, and between them they could not seem to get the garbage out. In the home where she grew up, her father had always done that job. In his home, his mother had taken out the garbage. So week after week in their home the garbage mounted until it spilled on the floor before it was taken out. Each was waiting for the other to take responsibility for it. She was whispering under her breath: "What's wrong with him? Men always take out the garbage." And he was complaining, "How can she let the garbage go like that?"

Garbage may not be the problem in your marriage, but most marital problems come down to the same kind of issue: we go around muttering to ourselves about all the things our mates should do but don't, and the things they do but shouldn't. Each one is sure everybody would be better off if the *other* would just listen to him.

One wife says: "My father always remembered to do such romantic things at holidays. He used to send mother flowers and leave little notes on her pillow. My husband forgot our anniversary this year and gave me bumperguards for the Volkswagen for Christmas." A husband complains: "I planned on marrying a woman who was a gourmet cook. I thought we'd be eating capon under glass by candlelight. But that's not my wife. She doesn't like to get much fancier than chicken noodle soup, and she even burns her bake-and-serve rolls."

You see? Part of you may disapprove just a little of the mate you married, and sometimes that disapproval may be for very good reasons. Your partner may not, in fact, live up to your highest ideals on all accounts. His or her preferences may not always match what you imagine to be good taste. It is even possible that your spouse has a flaw that is genuine — a weakness in anybody's view, not just compared to your idea of perfection.

But if you are to have a marriage where love thrives, you must accept your mate totally, just as he or she is, and not plan any renovation. Nobody ever changes anybody else, but many cause great suffering by trying.

One of the happiest marriages I've ever seen was that of a very slim woman and her rather obese husband. It was very important to her to control her weight, and she was careful to count calories — but she never counted anybody's but her own. I noted with amazement that she did not make an issue of weight with her husband — she never nagged him, she never teased him, she never acted superior or looked for any subtle way to say, "Trim down, Fats!" She simply loved him.

Once when someone asked her about her husband's weight problem, she said this: "He knows he's too heavy. The mirror tells him so every day. He doesn't need me to remind him too. What he needs is someone to make him feel wonderful, hopeful, worthwhile."

I'd say that was a lady who understood what love is about. Don't we all need someone to make us feel wonderful, to share our hopes, to reaffirm our value as human beings? Don't you wish your mate, the person closest to you in the whole world, would do just that for you — regardless of what your flaw is?

Accept your mate for the person he or she is. Love your partner unconditionally, no matter what his or her personality set or fault or weakness may be. Concentrate on those strengths that attracted you in the first place. At one time that spouse of yours was the most appealing creature on earth to you — his or her good points bowled you over and delighted you, and they can again if you give your attention to them rather than to the negative discoveries you've made.

Let your partner know that he or she has your approval. Give your support and enthusiasm. Find a way to say, "You're okay." The man who wanted his wife to prepare capon under glass finally gave up his perfected image and accepted the real person he'd married, and he found out that she really wanted to be a writer, not a gourmet cook. So he quit buying her crepe pans and got her a typewriter, a gesture that united them in mutual appreciation.

One of nature's great truths is that people flourish with approval. Criticism, frowning silence, nagging — even when they are for a person's own good — can draw life and hope out of the best of us, withering self-esteem and destroying relationships. But unconditional love, nonrestrictive acceptance and approval, can nourish any soul into bloom. You've heard this saying: "Accept me as I am, so I may learn what I can become." Only the people who feel the wholehearted and genuine support of those who love them *as they are* have the ability to grow into their full potential.

Ironic as it may seem, the best way to change the one you love is not to try. He or she may change independently, but not without the security of your love *now*. Remember all the reasons you chose your husband or wife in the first place, acknowledge the good that you see in him or her, allow that person to grow and improve in the direction of the highest and best unfolding of the individual he or she was meant to be. Remember to be loyal to the person you love most — to give your love and encouragement, your loyal support, not to some ideal in your head but to that real partner you share life with.

Persistence

Part 5

Press Forward

Do you remember your childhood dream for yourself? In your first dream, what did you see as a goal? Were you going to be Miss America? a great athlete? President of the United States? Superman? I know a seven-year-old who was told that O. J. Simpson was retiring from football and responded by saying, "I'd like to take his job." In the innocent eyes of the very young, nothing is impossible. We all once thought we were surely going to be somebody.

But those dreams have a way of fading, don't they? Life's discouragements interfere, we fail at some endeavor, our self-confidence wanes; eventually we give up, we relinquish the dream. We may call it facing reality or coming to know our own limitations, but it's quitting all the same.

And quitting is wrong. It's the only sure way to fail; because as long as you keep trying, you still have a chance. Maybe by now you've given up on Superman; probably your present dreams concern school and careers and family — and perhaps even athletics or politics still. Nevertheless, there is only one way to make them come true — by believing in them enthusiastically and pursuing them daily. The secret is to keep going, even when you have setbacks. Who is to say that the day you stop trying isn't the day before you succeed?

My little seven-year-old friend was happy to volunteer for Simpson's job because he saw O. J. as a success. Do you think he considered all the passes Simpson has missed or the pain he has suffered or the sacrifices he's made? Of course not, and neither do we, really, because all that is history. But there was a time when it was present tense and very real, and nobody knew it but O. J. himself. You know, if he had quit after a grueling and discouraging college game, we'd never have heard about him at all. Then the effort *would* have been wasted. To make anything pay off, you have to keep at it.

Consider Babe Ruth, another great athlete. What was he famous for? Home runs: 714 of them. Do you know how many times he suffered the humiliation of striking out? One thousand, three hundred and thirty times — almost double his number of home runs.

Let me tell you the story of a 1927 baseball game played at Shibe Park in Philadelphia. The Babe came up to bat and fanned it once, twice, three times: he was out. At his next turn he struck out again, leaving two runners on base; and 35,000 fans booed and jeered as he returned to the dugout. When he came up next, in the eighth inning, the pressure was on. The Athletics were ahead three to one, and the bases were loaded, with two outs. The Yankees' winning run was on base, and there was no other chance to bat it in: the game depended on Ruth, who stepped to the plate already a loser for the day. He'd struck out twice that afternoon, and everybody knew it; the crowd was letting him know what they thought. Nobody deserves to have to take such abuse; anybody would have understood if he'd refused to bat under that kind of pressure.

But Babe Ruth hung in there. He stepped to the plate, steadied himself, watched the first pitch come. It was good. He swung, and he missed. Strike one. The next pitch was good too. Babe put all his power into his swing. He missed again, and his own momentum brought him to the ground. Through the cloud of dust his fall had raised, he heard the umpire shout, "Strike two!" Again Ruth steadied himself at the plate. Again the pitch was fast and accurate. Again Babe swung, and this time he connected, hitting that ball clear out of the park.

That's the difference between a champ and a rookie — the champ has staying power. The champ doesn't bemoan his failures; he goes on trying until he succeeds.

Here is another example of a champ, this one a politician. He failed in business in '31; he was defeated for the legislature in '32. He failed again at business in '33; and he was elected to the legislature in '34. He ran for speaker in '38 and lost; he ran for a place in the electoral college in '40 and lost; he ran for Congress in '43 and lost. In '46 he was elected to Congress; but in '48 he was defeated. In '55 he ran for the Senate and lost; he was defeated for vice-president in '56; and he lost another Senate election in '58. Not much of a record, is it? Who would blame a fellow for giving up after all that? Nobody. Nobody, because nobody would ever have heard of him. If he had not pushed ahead, if he had not entered another election, if he had not tried again, nobody would have cared. But he did run again. And in 1860 Abraham Lincoln, whose record I have just given you, was elected president of the United States. His dream wasn't much different from dozens of other men's, but his came true because he wouldn't quit.

You mustn't quit either — not on your dreams for this week or this year or even this lifetime. The *next* lifetime depends on your seeing this one through. The Lord put it this way:

"Wherefore, ye must press forward with a steadfastness in Christ, having a perfect brightness of hope, and a love of God and of all men. Wherefore, if ye shall press forward, feasting upon the word of Christ, and endure to the end, behold, thus saith the Father: Ye shall have eternal life." (2 Nephi 31:20.)

Press forward. It's not just a piece of nice advice; it's a commandment. Press forward — one step at a time, always believing that you can do a great and excellent work here on this earth and that your life matters, maybe more than you imagine. Progression is an eternal law: obey it today and tomorrow and the next day by continuing to try, by viewing failures as challenges to meet and never as signals to quit. Don't allow yourself to be one of the nameless ones who almost made it. Your childhood vision was true. You *are* somebody, and you can have all the success you earn by pressing forward.

The Power of a Daily Routine

Alice, when she was in Wonderland, once found herself running forward in order to keep from going back. No matter how hard she ran, she was not able to progress—only to keep from regressing. It's a sensation we all have experienced, and to describe it our language includes such common phrases as "running around in circles" and "being on a treadmill."

Often we get so involved in expending energy, in hurrying, in busying ourselves that we neglect to focus on a goal. What is all the fuss *for*? Is it enough that we are "anxiously engaged"—or should we evaluate our busyness in terms of its purpose?

I think we do confuse velocity with virtue much too often. And the secret to correcting this error is a simple shift in perspective: in order to progress, we need to give attention not to hurry but to habit. Those who surpass themselves each day are those who have made their habits work for them, not against them.

Think about it for a minute: as you fly through life, how many of those automatic habitual things that you do have real purpose? And how many of them are meaningless motion? Consider how much time and energy you would have if you could eliminate those routines that have no reason. Further, think how nice it would be if the tasks you know you *should* accomplish each day came automatically. All it takes is paying a little attention to your habits so that you are in charge of them instead of the other way around.

Here's an example: brushing your teeth. Every morning you brush your teeth first thing—you don't have to think about it, you don't worry about it, you just do it; and you reap the benefits whenever you see the dentist. Is there any reason why developing character traits should be harder than developing strong teeth? Of course not. You can make it a habit to think of something good about each person you meet or to look for some way to give to him. The key to making your daily routine work for you is to make a conscious choice as to which habits you want to have and then to practice, practice, practice them. Soon they become automatic, and then being your best self is easy.

Suppose you decide you want to play the piano beautifully. You don't hop out of bed one morning, say "Today's the day," and spend twelve hours at the piano making it all come true. You know you can't get from Chopsticks to Chopin in one session, no matter how long the session is. Learning to play well requires repeated practice sessions, and so does learning to live well. Set your goals high, but build behavior habits toward them one day at a time, repeating each day your practice of whatever trait you're trying to develop.

Finally, it is important to be consistent. You've heard people say: "I can quit smoking any time—it's easy. And I should know, because I've already quit sixteen times!" Anybody can take the first step in building or breaking a habit, but the one who succeeds is the person who takes the second and third steps and who keeps plodding along until it becomes second nature to him.

I used to play professional baseball, and I noticed that as I went into spring training I had to be regular in my physical training habits if my body was to perform the way I wanted it to. I noticed that even if I had had a good record the year before, I couldn't walk out in April and say, "Look out, crowd, I'm a twenty-game winner!" My body wasn't ready. It had to be developed all over again.

As I went through the arduous task of performing on the field to get muscles and coordination ready for the opening game, I noticed that it usually required about three weeks to get into condition. Until a ball player invests time regularly every day, he can't produce physically.

And until you invest time every day in an area of personal progress that you have mapped out for yourself, you can't produce spiritually. You're heading no place; and it doesn't matter how fast you're moving, because there is no real goal.

The mind and spirit do work very much like the body in this regard. Did you ever try to go on a diet? Well, there is a physical phenomenon that sets in at age thirty that demands that you pay attention to what you eat. When I was playing ball, I couldn't get any heavier than 165 pounds — even if I ate five meals a day and lots of malts and pastries in between.

I had a brother six years my senior who was really skinny and quite a bit smaller in stature. Then at age thirty something happened to him. He just — whiftt — bulked right up. I used to rib him — you know how younger brothers will do. I suggested that he get a job with Goodyear as an understudy for the blimp.

He patted me on the head and said: "Go ahead and laugh. One day you are going to be thirty."

"Not I. No, I weigh 165 pounds, and I'll stay this way all my life!"

Then my thirtieth birthday came. They brought in the cake (all the family had gathered) and had me blow out the candles. I did. Then — whiftt — I went out too. Soon I was up to 205.

As I got a little older, I finally did as most people do — I vowed I would get on a diet and get back to my playing weight. I wanted to look like an all-American athlete. I got on a program, but for the first two weeks — nothing. I'd starve myself, I'd exercise, I'd go through more programs than you can imagine, and I'd get on the scale — 205. I decided it didn't work. So I quit. But if I had just stayed at it for one more day or two more days, until my diet had become a matter of habit, I would have had results.

If you can do anything for twenty-one days in a row, you can do it for a lifetime. Remember this. It is consistency that brings you personal power. If you are on again and off again in your efforts, you may never reach your goals.

Those who have transcended the diminished life that most of us follow are those who have learned the power of a daily routine.

If they want to be scripture readers, for instance, they read every day — and, more important, at the same time every day; not today in the morning and tomorrow at noon. They have found that there is efficacy in this kind of routine. They have found that perfection is achieved day by day. A rut is very different from a routine. A rut takes you deeper and deeper; a routine takes you higher and higher if it be a righteous one.

Habit is powerful. It invites us to act automatically. What begins as a faint pattern to our activities can solidify into concrete-and-steel forms for our lives. If we are careful to choose and develop good habits, we can put that power to work for us, helping us build day by day, regularly and consistently, the kinds of traits that will exalt us. Never let life's pressures push you into habits that keep you busy for nothing; instead, take command of your life by controlling your habits.

New Year, New You

In the middle of his introduction of a "lovely ninety-one-year-old lady" who was to speak next, the program's master of ceremonies felt a hand on his arm. He stopped short and turned to find the speaker in question already at his side. "Not so fast," she said, loudly enough for the microphone to pick up and carry her voice. "I'm not *that* old; I'm only ninety!"

I like this woman's spirit. A year is a good-sized chunk of time, and it can make a big difference in your life regardless of whether it is your seventeenth, your twenty-fifth, your fortieth or your sixty-seventh year. Often when I hear people protest that they are too old to begin some project or to learn some new skill, I think of the woman who began ballet lessons at thirty-six years of age. "Well," she reasoned, "thirty-six is pretty old to be starting, and I probably won't ever be a performer. But I've always wanted to learn this; and if I put it off longer, I'll just have to start older. Next year I'll be thirty-seven no matter what—I might as well be thirty-seven and dancing."

Time does have a way of passing, and it is up to us to determine whether we will take advantage of that motion or simply let time pass us by. Reflect for a moment on the year just past. Who were you a year ago? Haven't the experiences of those twelve months altered you in some way?

Let's face it: change is inevitable in life. If you doubt it, pull out a scrapbook and check out the clothes and haircut you were sporting a few seasons ago. Consider that it hasn't been long since we had no vaccines or frozen foods. Think how recently we acquired television and space travel. Remember when we thought fifty cents was expensive for a gallon of gasoline?

The world changes, life changes, and we change too. The big question is this: Are you changing in the manner you desire for yourself? Are you charting the direction of your personal change, or are you being shoved toward some goal you didn't choose for yourself? Do you see yourself progressing steadily from the you of a year ago toward the person you want to become? Are your ideals any closer to realities now than they were last year? Or has the pressure of life blurred your purpose, leaving you content to tread water and barely stay afloat? Too often we lose our resolve and settle for survival in place of conquering.

Survival is an instinct — all creatures respond to it. But man has the divine power to reason, to plan, to carve out his future with a purpose. As Henry David Thoreau pointed out, man may fail or prevail in his thoughts alone. And Steve Covey expanded on that idea in his book *Spiritual Roots of Human Relations* to suggest that every crisis in life is preceded by thought and resolution — for every Calvary there is a Gethsemane where the outcome is determined by a man's pondering, deciding, and proceeding with a plan.

There is a Persian legend that tells of a hunchback prince who sought to stand straight and tall. He had built for him a statue of himself as he imagined himself — square, determined shoulders; head held high; body erect. Every day the prince stood before the statue and held himself as nearly like it as he could. Eventually he became as tall and straight as his dream.

Now, I don't mean to suggest by this story that everything we aim for will be ours. But I am certain that we cannot attain what we do not aim for. Since every year of our lives surely brings change, shouldn't we employ our God-given power to direct that change?

An earthworm survives by instinct. And it is instinct as well that draws the earthworm up out of the ground during a rainstorm and leaves him to die on the sidewalk. But you are not a creature of instinct; you need not merely survive. You can conquer by choosing the direction of your changes for next year and following that direction by intellect and will.

Those who are most successful in life are those who live by this principle, who plan and reason and thereby control the motion of their time. Look around. You can see that the happiest marriages are those in which both partners actively think of ways to build their love and unity rather than letting the relationship slide along on its own. The happiest children are those whose parents think hard about the sort of experiences and teaching they will have at home rather than allowing "nature to take its course." In such cases, nature's course runs downhill; the wise parent chooses and follows his own course.

I think we can agree that setting and reaching goals is important, but a yearly assessment is quite different from the daily effort of making it work. Let me suggest two ideas to help keep that long-term plan in motion from day to day. First of all, if we do not control our direction, the greater things in life are at the mercy of the smaller things. Consider the father whose goal is to develop close relationships with his family. If he does not plan specific steps in that direction, he finds that less important things take up the time and energy he needs for his larger goal. His job is demanding and leaves him exhausted in the evening. He arrives home with no specific idea about how he will spend time with the kids, so he sits down in front of the television, switches off his weary mind, and zap! — today's little issues prevent the realization of the year's goal. Unless we concentrate on making the days add up to a fruitful year, they run away with it, leaving us 365 purposeless pockets of empty time.

The second idea is a tough one to accept all the time, but it is most important at those moments when we most want to reject it. It is the notion of personal responsibility. We are the only ones who can create or lose our dreams. There is no point in blaming fate or circumstance for our lives' courses: we choose how we will respond to each circumstance; we are accountable to ourselves at all times.

We design ourselves and our lives in thought. Do you find, for example, that a certain series of events or thoughts brings out the worst in you? Then you must break the chain of events, change the pattern of thought. No one else can do this for you. Does a certain set of ideas break down your courage and make you despair? You, then, are the one who must thrust them aside. You alone determine what you think, how you plan, and therefore what you are.

Each January first begins a new year, a year that will surely bring a new you. Twelve months from then you will have changed, and that day is the time to resolve what the nature of that change will be. Then — and this may be just as difficult — the next day and the day after and every tomorrow all year long, you must renew your resolve and take responsibility for making it come true.

The story is told that when Henry Ward Beecher was a boy, he attended the kind of school where the students stood to recite or to respond in class. On one particular day the master asked a simple enough question to which a boy gave what appeared to the others to be a good answer. But the schoolmaster glared at the boy and told him to sit down. The next boy he called on gave much the same answer and was also commanded to be seated. Several boys in succession received the same confusing disapproval of the only answer any of them could think of. Finally Beecher was called upon, but when the master roared at him to sit down after he had answered the question, Beecher stood his ground and insisted that he was correct. The master challenged him again; Beecher did not budge. Then a smile broke over the master's face and he said, "It seems that all of you had the correct answer, but only Beecher was certain enough to stay with it."

This year, be certain enough of your own direction to stay with it. Don't act out of instinct, don't let circumstances or the motion of time carry you along. You were meant to shape your own future by your wits. Take control and do so, creating the new person you want to become each day of the year.

Virtue Its Own Reward

If you have ever gone shopping for the man or woman on your Christmas list who has everything, you know how frustrating it can be to try to find a suitable gift. To ease this kind of frustration, some merchants offer such items as sterling silver contact lens cases and engraved toothbrushes. Bloomingdale's once advertised a mink jogging outfit, and I have seen a catalog offering a Texas-shaped swimming pool filled with Perrier water. Of course, such items are astronomically expensive, and most of us dream up other ways to solve our shopping dilemmas, dismissing such suggestions as extravagant. What would you do with a mink sweat suit, anyway?

Even though few of us expect to give or receive these kinds of super-luxuries, we all would like our rewards. In fact, we expect them. We work in anticipation of a paycheck, and our sense of justice suggests to us that it is only fair for us to receive some form of recognition for our other good deeds.

But sometimes our idea of the kind or amount of recognition we deserve is not in harmony with what we actually get. For example, picture the two nine-year-old boys who were on their way home from school. As they walked along they spotted a wallet lying near the curb. Looking through it, they found a twenty-dollar bill and an identification card giving an address in the neighborhood. As they started toward the address, their minds filled with visions of chocolate sundaes and maybe even terrific skateboards. They had no notion of keeping the money they'd found, but they knew what they'd do with the generous reward they'd receive for their honesty.

They found the house, rang the bell, and gave the wallet to the woman who answered the door. She was delighted to see it and very grateful. She praised the boys and thanked them, giving them each a squeeze. The boys remained expectantly on the front porch. Sensing that they thought something more was coming, the woman told the boys what concern she'd had over the lost wallet and thanked them again. When she finally closed the door, the two boys started dejectedly on their way; and as they reached the sidewalk, one turned to the other and said, "The squeeze didn't do it."

How often do you feel that way? You perform a great act of Christian charity and find yourself disappointed with your reward. Or you struggle to be obedient—to study the scriptures, pay your tithing, do your genealogical research, work at the stake farm—and you never seem to get the chances you need, you can't seem to get far enough ahead to replace your ancient car or paint the house, and you never get enough time to play with the kids. And all this time the family across the street ignores the Lord's commandments and prospers—*they* can afford to pack their kids into their new four-wheel-drive RV, hitch their twenty-foot boat to the back, and take the kids on a three-week tour of the national parks. Where is the justice in that?

Those who stand before the Lord and say, "I've been good—now bless me," are missing full comprehension of what the Lord intends for us. Mortality isn't a cosmic-sized version of *Let's Make a Deal*—we don't trade good deeds for blessings; we can't buy prosperity with obedience. The Lord sees further than this for us. He has given us commandments which can help us cope in this sphere and which are also rewards for us themselves as we obey them. Our obedience to celestial law not only governs our behavior, it builds us into celestial people—it gives us those tremendous strengths of character which can improve us and carry us higher eternally.

Here's an analogy. Any of us can study enough to pass a test; any of us can practice enough to hit one golf ball; any of us can follow along and pick out a tune—we get lucky or we make a special effort, and we are able to do any number of things one time. But that doesn't make us scholars or golfers or pianists—one shot doesn't make an expert. In order to be reliably good at anything, you have to give yourself over to it and make it a part of you.

The matter of being virtuous is the same. The occasional kind thought, generous deed, fervent prayer, or impulse to forgive does not constitute a Christian life. We can become Christlike only by practicing his principles consistently and sincerely. And our motivation in this practice must be simply to serve one another with love—no other reason for doing good is like Christ's, so any other reason makes the act empty.

C. S. Lewis, in his book *Mere Christianity*, suggests that each time you make a choice it alters your inner self; so you shape your soul by your choosings. Each decision to do or say the unkind thing not only makes you a doer of evil, it also contributes to turning the central, essential you into what Lewis calls "a hellish creature." Similarly, each decision to do good not only makes you a doer of good, it also helps build your inner self into a Godlike creature—one that can associate in peace and harmony with God and with other people, one that can be at peace with itself.

If we want to become celestial beings, doesn't it make sense that we should develop our celestial essence? Obedience to the Lord's laws is the way to do that. In this way the old saying is really true: virtue *is* its own reward. Our reward for being virtuous is that that practice of Christian behavior transforms us into Christlike beings.

The key is in motivation: the fine line between what you *do* and what you *are* is determined by your reasons for acting. Jesus Christ never gave with the question in mind of receiving glory— that was the adversary's plan.

May you give for the joy of giving, may you serve for the opportunity to serve, may you love and learn and share for the sake of loving, learning, sharing. In short, may you live virtuously purely to become virtuous, and may you realize the rewards of such living.

Sleeping When the Wind Blows

Let me share with you a fine story made popular some years back:

"Many years ago the old country fair in parts of England was, besides being the place of exhibition for farm products, where employer and employee met. A farmer here sought his help for the coming year, and young and old went to the fair to be employed.

"Farmer Smith wanted a boy to work on his farm. He was doing some interviewing of candidates. A thoughtful-looking lad of about sixteen attracted him. The boy was confronted with a rather abrupt question from the gruff old agriculturist. 'What can you do?' The boy swung back at him in the same style, 'I can sleep when the wind blows.'

"It was no wonder at all that the farmer turned right-about-face to others for the help he needed on receiving such an answer. Notwithstanding he didn't particularly like the answer to a civil question he got from the teenager, there was something about the gray eyes of that fellow that got under his skin.

"He approached the lad again with the same question, 'What did you say you could do?' Again the same answer bounced back at him, 'I can sleep when the wind blows.'

"Mr. Smith was still disgusted with such an answer and went to other parts of the fair to look into the faces of other youngsters who might want a job on a farm, but there was something about the answer he got that stuck to him like glue. First thing he knew his feet were carrying him back to meet the steady gaze of those deliberate eyes of the boy with such strange language.

" 'What did you say you could do?' for the third time he thundered at the farm help. For the third time, too, the farmer got the same answer, 'I can sleep when the wind blows.'

" 'Get into the wagon — we'll try you out.'

"Now, according to the story we don't hear very much about our boy and how he was getting along with his new employer for several weeks, but we can guess pretty accurately that his time had been occupied pretty well.

"One night Farmer Smith was wakened about 2:00 A.M. with what might be a cyclone. It seemed that gusts from the north in only a few minutes developed with intensity to threaten the roof over his head. The trees cracked and noises outside turned the nervous system of our friend upside down. The speed he used to jump into his trousers was only outdone by the lightning as it broke up the darkness outside. With shoes half-laced he rushed out into the farmyard to see if anything on the premises was still intact, but he would need the services on a wicked night like this of that new boy. He called up the stairs of the attic where the latter slept, but the response was the healthy lung heaving of a healthy lad. He went half the way up the stairs and thundered again, but only a snore echoed back. In excitement he went to the boy's bed and did everything but tear the bed clothes from the youth, but the lad slept on.

"With a mixture of desperation and disgust he faced the gale, and out into the farmyard he plunged. He first approached the cow barn. Lo and behold, the milk producers were peacefully chewing their cuds, and the inside of their abode was as snug as a mouse under a haystack. It didn't take him long to discover how the boy had chinked up the cracks of the cow abode and reestablished the locks and hinges. In the pigpen he found the same tranquility, notwithstanding the forces at work that night.

"He turned to the haystack. As he felt about in the darkness, it didn't take him very long to determine again the preparation of the lad with the gray, steady eyes. Every few feet on that feedstack wires had been thrown and weighted on each side. With this construction the alfalfa was peacefully under control and laughing at the elements.

"Our farmer friend was stunned with what revelations he had in a few minutes of that cyclone night. He dropped his head. His mental maneuvers shot like lightning to the boy snoring in the attic. Again, the peculiar answer of a few weeks ago slapped him in the face: 'I can sleep when the wind blows.' " (Marvin O. Ashton, *To Whom It May Concern* [Bookcraft, 1964], pp. 102-104.)

Can you sleep when the wind blows? Are you sufficiently prepared for life's trials, for the real storms of tragedy, that you can not only survive but do so securely and serenely? You can be if you maintain a close relationship with the Lord.

Jesus Christ taught an interesting parable about storms. He said that a certain wise man built his house upon a rock. "And the rain descended, and the floods came, and the winds blew, and beat upon that house; and it fell not: for it was founded upon a rock." Now, it seems there was another man who was not so wise: he had built his house on the sand. "And the rain descended, and the floods came, and the winds blew, and beat upon that house; and it fell: and great was the fall of it." (Matthew 7:25, 27.)

The truths taught here are powerful and perhaps quite frightening as well. Notice that *both* houses were subjected to rain and floods and wind—the difference between them was not the amount or kind of weather they experienced, the difference was how they withstood that weather. Just as neither house in the parable escaped the storm, none of us will be able to avoid life's storms. We can count on being blasted from time to time by losses, disappointments, pains. But if we are properly prepared, if we are close to the Lord, we can also count on weathering any trial.

Sometimes it is not a major crisis that gets us down; often the steady stream of day-to-day troubles causes erosion in our spirits. We all know what it is to have a bad day. We are used to hearing the expression, "I've got some good news and some bad news"; and sometimes life is like hearing that you didn't get a parking ticket—but your car's been stolen. Not one of us gets away without any bad news. We get discouraged. We have a bill we can't pay, we run just a yard of concrete short for the new carport, we feel unloved and ignored by those whose approval we crave.

I know one man who decided when he got up one morning that through that entire day he would not let anything upset him, no matter how miserable it was. He did well too. He didn't yell when his daughter spilled milk on his suit at the breakfast table. He didn't tear at his hair when he ran out of gas on the way to work. He didn't moan when the fellow next to him got the promotion he was expecting. But you should have seen him punch the candy machine when he lost his quarter. Enough is enough.

Don't you sometimes feel that way about the adversity you face? Wouldn't it be nice if we could just yell, "Uncle!" and have life's heartaches let up? But the system just doesn't work that way. We have to go on; no one has the power to halt adversity.

We do, however, have the power to cope and to strengthen ourselves so we are *ready* to cope when we have to. There are those who buckle under pressure, who fall apart when things get rough. They cannot sleep when the wind blows, as that young farmhand could, because they have not developed their faith. They have not chinked up their hearts against despair; they have not trusted in the Lord and learned that, no matter how dark the night or severe the storm, he can protect them.

But you, you know better than to leave yourself vulnerable. You know how to prepare to face great griefs and daily hassles with your hand in the Lord's. Disappointment will not have power to tear you apart, tragedy will not destroy you if you are certain of his protection. Even when a cyclone blows round your heart, he can whisper peace to your soul.

May you rest secure in his care. May you be prepared and peaceful in the face of life's storm, protected by your faith.

Endure to the End

A colleague of mine was passing a furniture store when a sign in the window caught his eye. It said: Finishers Wanted. Now, I suppose in the furniture business there is always a need for a finisher, but isn't that a sign that could apply almost anywhere? Finishers Wanted. The world has an ample supply of starters, but finishers are a rare breed.

It is so easy to start any project, to take the first step up the mountain road, to dream a big dream. But the world doesn't belong to those who start out brilliantly. It belongs to those who endure to the end. As the Lord said, "If they endure unto the end they shall be lifted up at the last day." (1 Nephi 13:37.) The message is simple: hold on even when the world would jolt you loose from your dream. Why? Because regardless of the outcome —whether you win or lose—there seems to be something about endurance itself, long-suffering, endurance to the end of the trial, that ennobles the human spirit as little else can.

There is not one of us who will not face hazard, disappointment, perhaps grave trial, as he pursues his life's quest. The pricks and thorns of existence may at times bruise our flesh until we bleed. You may feel that way even now. What are you to do at such a time? Give up? Retreat from the world in bitterness? Turn your back on the Lord and call all prayers unanswered? Many do. Sometimes they call themselves "realists" and say: "I should have known all the time. Life was not meant for high pursuit. I was not meant to be more than average." Do you know what I call these "realists"? I call them quitters. They didn't have the fire to finish what they started in life. They let trouble beat them down.

Bryant S. Hinckley once said: "There is no more searching test of the human spirit than the way it behaves under adversity, under long periods of struggle, disappointment and poverty. . . . Trouble strips a man of all his borrowed faith, reveals the strength and fiber of his soul, makes him acquainted with his own weakness and his own strength."

But those of us intent on life don't want trouble. We aren't anxious for a searching test of our human spirit. We just want to live good lives and be about our tasks. Have you ever found yourself praying to the Lord in this manner: "Please make this trial go away. Let it evaporate into the air. Ease my burden. Remove this bitter cup. And please do it now." And, of course, the next discovery is that the Lord doesn't do just what we ask. He lets us endure—if needs be, he lets us endure clear to the end.

Wrote Macdonald: "No words can express how much the world owes to sorrow. Most of the Psalms were born in a wilderness. Most of the Epistles were written in a prison. . . . The greatest poets have learned in suffering what they taught in song. . . . Take comfort, afflicted Christian! When God is about to make pre-eminent use of a man, He puts him in the fire. To which we all want to answer—take me out!"

James Talmage, a scholar and writer, said that to do his concentrated research and study he had to find a retreat other than his comfortable office or his study at home. He finally found an upper room in the tower of a large building, well removed from the noise and confusion of the city streets. There he spent many peaceful and busy hours with only one kind of intruder—the flying insects which would visit him when the windows were open in the summertime. Those self-invited guests were not unwelcome. Many times he would lay down his pen and, forgetting his studies, watch with interest the activities of his winged friends.

One day a wild bee from the neighboring hills flew into this upper room, and at intervals during an hour or more the scholar caught the hum of its flight. The little creature realized that it was a prisoner, yet all its efforts to find the exit through the partly opened casement failed. When James Talmage at last was ready to close up the room and leave, he threw the window wide open and at first tried to guide and then to drive the bee to liberty and safety, knowing well that if left in the room it would die as other insects trapped there had perished in the dry atmosphere. But the more he tried to drive it out, the more determinedly did the bee oppose and resist his efforts. The bee's peaceful hum developed into an angry roar, its daring flight became hostile and threatening.

Then suddenly the bee caught James Talmage off guard and stung his hand — the hand that would have guided it to freedom. It then alighted on a pendant attached to the ceiling, and the man left the room and the little creature which by now had sealed its own fate. Three days later he returned to the room and found the dried, lifeless body of the bee on the writing table. It had paid for its stubbornness with its life.

Now, to the bee's short-sightedness and selfish misunderstanding James Talmage had been a foe, a persistent persecutor, a mortal enemy bent on its destruction; while in truth he was its friend, striving to redeem it — in spite of itself — from the death that surely awaited it in the upper room with a window closed. (Retold from "The Parable of the Unwise Bee," *Improvement Era*, November 1962, p. 817.)

Are we so much wiser than the bee as we contend against the trials that come our way in life? Isn't it just possible that what we view as our deepest suffering may, in fact, be the manifestation of the Lord's very love for us? It is only, after all, in the extremities of our existence, with all the insignificant and unimportant details burned away, that we can truly come to know the Lord.

There is a cemetery on a hill in an arid Utah town that shelters against the desert wind four unforgettable little markers. They are not marble, nor are they engraved with fine writing. The family who erected them could not afford such extravagance. No, they are squares of cement that were written in with a stick while they were still wet. And their message is simple: "Here lies the child of John and Mary Thomas, died 1875," reads the first one. "Here lies the child of John and Mary Thomas, died 1876," reads the second. The third and fourth are like the first two. The message is stark, but the experience in human suffering must have been profound. As one looks at these markers, he cannot help but ask how John and Mary Thomas bore up under the sorrow of losing four small babies in their desert home. Did they become embittered, grim, give up on life, and call it dead? Or did they endure to the end with their hands in the Lord's? How did they finish the fight? Because, of course, finish they did. John and Mary Thomas have decades ago joined their children, and now all the suffering is but a memory.

Did they endure to the end or did they simply whimper and fade away? I don't know what happened to them, but I do have great hopes for what will happen to you and me. Through all of life's adversity, whatever we are called upon to endure, may we find the inner strength and the trust in the Lord to finish as brilliantly as we start.

Lay Aside Every Weight

If you want special treatment, go on a diet. Today's dieter has offered to him special books, special clubs, special menus at restaurants, special vitamins, special milk, even special TV dinners and junk food. I am about to add to this list of specials one more item: the dieter's scripture. Do you know it? It's found in Paul's Epistle to the Hebrews: "Let us lay aside every weight, . . . and let us run with patience the race that is set before us." (Hebrews 12:1.)

Lay aside every weight. Now, you and I know that Paul was not referring to a physical weight problem, but I think the analogy is a good one. That scriptural chapter goes on to talk about the way God chastens us, and to encourage us to accept challenges and go on, setting aside those habits and faults which would prevent us. Physical overweight is not so different from carrying spiritual burdens: extra pounds make every step an effort, the heart works harder, even breathing is more difficult. Life can easily become a discouraging struggle when your body keeps shouting: "Take a break. Give up!"

But the scripture advises us (*all* of us — for who does not have the spiritual burden of some fault?) to run with patience. Not to rest up, but to *run* and *keep* running. In order to reach our personal goals we must run and never quit; we must endure, or we do not have a chance. I am convinced that it is endurance (or stubbornness, or patience — call it what you will) more than any other quality that makes people winners. Those who succeed are those who clench their teeth and hang in there even when they feel discouraged, even when there is little hope of reaching the goal at all.

George Johannesen shares this story of a winner as it was told to him by a friend:

"When I was a freshman in college, I had a classmate named Pete Cavallo, who wanted nothing more than to earn a letter in athletics. The trouble was he was too little. Barely five feet tall and weighing scarcely more than a hundred pounds, he hardly met the physical requirements of competitive sports. Nevertheless, he elected to try cross-country running. Evidently he thought that even a little horse (Cavallo, you know, means horse) might excel in the long run.

"In those days the cross-country runners came up over a hill, down into the stadium, and around the track to the finish line, just after the other events were over and before the spectators had left.

"Little Pete Cavallo ran hard, but he was outclassed from the start. He finished the race, but only long after the last spectator had left the stadium. The next year he did a little better, and by the third year he had improved so much that he came in while there were still some spectators.

"So it was that in his fourth and last year his name was heard frequently in the stadium: 'Sure do wish those little Cavallo legs could make it this year!' But nobody really thought they would.

"Nevertheless, when the other events were over, there was an aura of expectancy and hope about the stadium. All eyes were on the hill, hoping to see little Pete Cavallo come up first. When one of those big, longlegged runners came into view, a great sigh of disappointment, as of a slowly deflating balloon, escaped the crowd. Dejectedly, the spectators began to leave.

"But suddenly, there was little Pete driving up over the hill. The stadium became pandemonium. Everyone was shouting, 'Come on, Pete; come on, little horse!' For the moment, the winner was forgotten. It was as if little Pete Cavallo had come in first. And in a sense, perhaps he really was the winner, because some forty years later I still remember him, but I have forgotten the name of the runner who took first place." ("The 'Little Horse' Who Also Ran," *Ensign*, February 1975, p. 88.)

Pete never really won, but he certainly never lost, and the

reason is that he ran *with patience*—he kept at it. Of course it feels wonderful to come in first, to be the winner; but the apostle Paul doesn't speak in terms of winning life's race, he admonishes us to endure to the end.

The people we honor most are not necessarily those who've chalked up a string of easy victories; rather, they are the ones who have overcome hardship to grow and achieve and finish their personal races. It doesn't take much patience or strength to win time after time, but it does require tremendous stamina to get up every time you fall. Sometimes falling can be devastating; sometimes we lack the courage and the hope to struggle up from our knees.

But we are not without help. The Lord requires of us difficult tasks, but not impossible ones. Let me add the next line to Paul's statement: ". . . let us lay aside every weight, . . . and let us run with patience the race that is before us, looking unto Jesus the author and finisher of our faith." (Hebrews 12:1-2.) We are never alone, we are never without strength if we just rely on the Lord for the help he wants to give us.

Those who run this lifelong race with patience and courage are those who recognize their need for a higher power than their own. May I emphasize that fact by reminding you of a story of an eleven-year-old boy, Johnny Sylvester. Perhaps you don't remember his name; but I'm sure you do recognize the other character in the story, the czar of baseball, Babe Ruth.

The Babe was playing in the World Series. Johnny Sylvester was dying in a nearby hospital. In fact, Johnny was in a coma. He would come out of it long enough to ask, "Did Babe hit a homer today?" And when they would shake their heads negatively, he would lapse back into unconsciousness. Johnny needed the will to live; he needed the news of a Ruth home run. Sometimes, for a small boy, motivation can come in seemingly insignificant acts. I guess we adults are sometimes not so different.

Finally, Johnny's desperate parents sent a telegram to a friend in St. Louis. Perhaps he could interrupt Babe Ruth long enough to let him know of Johnny Sylvester. The Babe always had a tender spot in his heart for boys. He himself had spent his boyhood in an orphanage.

In a few hours a telegram came to Johnny's parents for Johnny. It read: "I'm going to knock a homer for you in Wednesday's game. Hold on for me, little partner." It was from Babe Ruth himself.

New strength came to Johnny immediately. Now he had something to live for. He waited for Wednesday — waited and hoped.

As the Babe walked to the plate on Wednesday, Johnny Sylvester was listening to his radio. Thousands of fans were screaming in the stands. It was bedlam. For just a moment Babe Ruth knelt down by the plate. It was a very unassuming act. Not a soul in the stands knew what it was all about, because they didn't know the story of Johnny Sylvester. They didn't know he was following the apostle Paul's counsel; he was praying to keep a promise to a sick boy. Not even the anxious relatives at Johnny's bedside knew what was happening. All they knew was a moment of intense silence over the radio — then a blast through the air that could almost be felt — and the pandemonium of the crowd. The Babe had hit a homer.

Johnny Sylvester could not cheer. He could not even clap his hands. He could only whisper: "He hit it, daddy, he hit it for me. That was my homer." Babe Ruth hit three homers in that game.

You were meant to run life's race with hope and confidence. And when all seems lost, you must know that it is possible to dig down into the very depths of the human soul and find the strength and inspiration of the Lord to power us on. God bless us to "run with patience the race" and to "look unto him" for the ability to do so.

Expectations

You may have seen a child open a stack of packages as tall as he is on Christmas morning and then, casting weary eyes around, ask, "Is that all?" His parents about that time may want to clobber him, but there is something almost universal in his question. We look forward to Christmas day with such bright dreams, believing so thoroughly that a rosy glow will break over our tired hearts, that nothing in the realm of reality could possibly measure up to our expectations. Didn't the Christmas tree smell more piney in some far-distant past? Weren't the lights more enchanting? "Is this all?" Some part of you may still ask, "Is this it?"

When such a thought crosses my mind at this season, I think back to that divine birth almost two thousand years ago. Could there have been a more humble arrival? For centuries men had looked to the coming of the Savior. They were expecting a champion who would raise them dramatically from the dust. As George Macdonald wrote:

> They all were looking for a king
> To slay their foes and lift them high;
> Thou cam'st, a little baby thing
> That made a woman cry.

They expected a political king to send oppressive governments toppling. They expected power in the world's sense — the kind of king they already knew, one who would reign with pomp and wealth. All those who had looked so long to the birth of this king wanted to be able to grind their enemies down to size, to conquer, to be at last on the side of the mighty instead of always being beaten by a world too big for them.

But how did Christ actually come? He came a helpless infant, born in a borrowed stable to parents in the humblest station in life. And all his life he little resembled an earthly king. His clothes were simple, his manner undramatic. He did not own a home, let alone a palace. He did not take up the sword to champion his cause. Those who followed him were not granted sudden wealth or power over their enemies; in fact, many of them were commanded to leave all worldly goods behind them. And when the confrontation test the Jewish nation had waited for came — when the question was how he would stand up against the mighty Roman government — he was again a disappointment. He did not come in with a blazing army to tear down the place and throw his enemies over. No. He submitted meekly to an unfair judgment and allowed himself to be crucified. In view of their expectation, it is not surprising that there were some who had waited all those years for the coming of Christ who responded, like that child at Christmas: "Is that all? Is this it?" They had been looking for something different.

But how right, how appropriate in every way, was the Savior's birth and life! Could he have understood our human lot if he had been beyond human concern? What if the mantle of glory had fallen upon him all at once? What if his birth had been a grandiose event accompanied by pomp and circumstance? Suppose a banner had been raised saying: "This is the Son of God." Would he then have been able to walk with us through our sometimes lonely and unrecognized lives? Could he then have said with real empathy, "I know," when we cry against our pain? You see, wherever we've been, whatever dark road we've walked along, whatever cause we've had to shiver in our fright, he's been there too. He knows what it is to be forsaken by friends, to have his best efforts mocked. He knows what it is to be hungry, to be tempted, to be so weary he could hardly take another step. Because he did not meet mankind's expectations of a king, when you kneel at the very limits of your endurance you may know for certain that Jesus has knelt there before you.

Endurance. Jenny Walker knew all about that as she trudged along the main street that led to Peterson's store. Winter had come early, and the cold, wet weather made Christmas a spectre in that depression year. Even though she was only thirty-two, Jenny felt like an old woman, her cares so burdensome that she seemed to feel their weight physically as well as mentally. Her husband had been gone a month now, out trying to find work with the construction crews along the highway. He had been a sheep man, but the hard times and the early winter had not been kind to them. They had watched their sheep drop dead one by one in the harsh climate, until their flock had been decimated. And with those sheep went their dreams — so much for youth's bright hopes.

"I think I can earn enough to meet the mortgage payments so we can at least keep the farm," David had said. Then he'd gone, leaving her and five children to make their way. She hadn't heard from him since. Was it just the mail? She knew how irregular the mail was at Christmas.

The bell over the door jingled merrily as Jenny walked into Peterson's store. It was Christmas itself inside, with the heavy smell of gingerbread and pine in the air, and with the electric excitement of the children who were clustered around the table in the center of the country store. This table that sat unnoticed under its display of farm tools or flour sacks during the rest of the year was the center of interest for the little town during the weeks just before Christmas. For then, just once a year, the store carried toys and displayed them for all to see.

The day the toys arrived, the children could hardly sit still in school. Some lucky one would get the news that the toys had arrived, and the word would spread like magic. Dolls with painted faces and painted hair could hardly be resisted; and maybe for some very lucky little girl there would be a doll with real hair that curled around her face. Tinkertoys and blocks and pocketknives whispered enticingly of all they could create in the hands of a little boy. Jenny watched the children "Ooh!" and "Ah!" and shine with excitement as they stood before the loaded table. And she caught a familiar face among them too: her own nine-year-old Tad was there wondering what he'd get for Christmas, just as excited and hopeful as the rest of them.

At that, Jenny had to turn her head quickly and blink back the tears to keep from crying. There was simply no money for Christmas this year — not enough for a twenty-five-cent doll to stick in a matchbox, not enough to buy the sugar to make honey candy. There was not enough money for the mortgage payment, and David was — she didn't know where. She traded the eggs she'd brought for some flour to make bread, and sadly she headed home. She was sure that there was no one more miserable than she on the face of the earth. "Oh, God, what have I ever done wrong that you would reject me so?" she prayed as she plodded through the snow. She wondered if her faith had always been misplaced. Certainly all her best efforts in life had come to nothing.

Christmas Eve brought a blizzard to the town where Jenny lived. Inside her home she built a fire and did her best to help the children sing Christmas carols and feel a sense of the season. But she could hardly bear it when Tad came running in with his stocking to hang by the fireplace, and the little ones followed along. "I don't think Santa can find us in this weather," she tried to say, looking at the five empty socks along the fireplace. "Santa can do anything," Tad had assured her, and he went to sleep with that same Christmas shine she had seen in his eyes at the store.

Jenny sat before the socks late into the night wondering what to do and where her family would go when they lost their farm. She tried to pray again but, concluding that maybe God was just too busy to bother with her, she fell asleep on the couch in front of the five limp little socks.

How long she'd been asleep she did not know, when she awoke to the sound of footsteps in the hall. Someone was inside her house. She had picked up a log to arm herself against the intruder when she heard the sweetest sound she'd ever known. "Jenny?" It was David's voice. "Oh, Jenny. I'm sorry. I would have done anything to get here sooner," he said. "But to get here at all I had to catch a ride with a trucker and then walk the last eight miles from the turnoff to town."

"I haven't heard from you for so long," Jenny whimpered.

"We don't have mail service along the road," he explained. "Did you think you were alone? Did you really think I'd ever leave you all alone?"

Jenny thought about that as she watched David put a small toy in each of the five socks and bring out a new pocketknife for Tad. But Jenny's Christmas gift was not a small one. It was the question repeated over and over in her head, "Did you think I'd ever leave you alone?" which seemed to be a message not just from her husband, but from the Lord himself. "You are never alone."

Let that be *your* Christmas message. You are never alone. When we are tempted to look for Christ to enter our lives in some dazzling way, when we expect him to come and crush our dragons, we may be looking for something that will not come. And, like the child at Christmas, we may end up disappointed, saying, "Is that all?" No, that is not all, unless glitter is all we look for. But if we look for his quiet love and understanding, we will not be disappointed. Christ came as a baby and walked the path of a man, suffering all the anguish of mortality, so that he may silently hold your hand when you walk your own rugged path. He is there to comfort you and raise you up even when your voice seems to echo back to you in the silence. Could a rich and glittering king ever have done that?

May we grow to understand what to expect of our Lord. At Christmas and throughout the year may we know all that he has provided for us. And may we truly, deeply appreciate its value.